Your
Horoscope
2022

....

Capricorn

22 December – 20 January

igloobooks

igloobooks

Published in 2021
First published in the UK by Igloo Books Ltd
An imprint of Igloo Books Ltd
Cottage Farm, NN6 0BJ, UK
Owned by Bonnier Books
Sveavägen 56, Stockholm, Sweden
www.igloobooks.com

0721 001
2 4 6 8 10 9 7 5 3 1
ISBN 978-1-80022-522-0

Written by Belinda Campbell and Denise Evans

Designed by Simon Parker
Edited by Natalie Graham

Printed and manufactured in China

CONTENTS

. . . .

INTRODUCTION
. . . .

This 15-month guide has been designed and written to give
a concise and accessible insight into both the nature of your
star sign and the year ahead. Divided into two main sections,
the first section of this guide will give you an overview of your
character in order to help you understand how you think,
perceive the world and interact with others, and – perhaps just
as importantly – why. You'll soon see that your zodiac sign
is not just affected by a few stars in the sky, but by planets,
elements, and a whole host of other factors, too.

The second section of this guide is made up of daily forecasts.
Use these to increase your awareness of what might appear on
your horizon so that you're better equipped to deal with the
days ahead. While this should never be used to dictate your life,
it can be useful to see how your energies might be affected or
influenced, which, in turn, can help you prepare for what life
might throw your way.

By the end of these 15 months, these two sections should
have given you a deeper understanding and awareness of
yourself and, in turn, the world around you. There are never
any definite certainties, but with an open mind you will find
guidance for what might be, and learn to take more control
of your own destiny.

THE CHARACTER OF
THE SEA GOAT

· · · · · · · · · · · · · · · · · ·

One small step for Capricorn can certainly be one giant leap for mankind when this determined sign gets its teeth into something. Whether it's dreaming of the stars like Capricorns Buzz Aldrin and Stephen Hawking or striving for first place like Tiger Woods, Capricorns are the earth signs of the calendar that can make their dreams a reality. Belonging to the tenth house of the zodiac calendar, where careers and vocations are key, the role that a disciplined Capricorn takes on, be it in business, science, or on the stage, can take them to dizzying heights of success. As an earth sign, tangible rewards can be essential to Capricorns — just look at their designer clothes, nice cars and beautiful houses — and if a Capricorn hasn't quite reached their goals yet, their dreams of grandeur will likely inspire them to only work harder.

Born with buckets of ambition, the Goat-symbolised Capricorn will not be satisfied with climbing mere ladders and will likely set themselves mountains to ascend. If the path they have taken is proving to be too rocky, rejection and failure can hit this prideful sign hard and any pain might be internalised due to their negative nature. Capricorns are pioneering cardinal characters and the world can be more than happy to dance to their Pied Piper tune. Just look at Calvin Harris, a Forbes-listed Capricorn recorded for being the highest paid DJ in the world for six consecutive years, showing how hardworking Capricorns can not only reach, but stay at the top of their profession. Status is of all importance to Capricorns, so being top dog, or Sea Goat rather, could be what helps drive this sign to the highest peaks of their success. Their top-of-the-podium attitude is perhaps why the number one and number two spots for the record amount of Formula 1 wins are both held by Capricorns: Lewis Hamilton and Michael Schumacher. Whatever their goals are, with authoritative Saturn ruling over Capricorn, this disciplined sign is sure to get results.

THE SEA GOAT

Often depicted as a mountain Goat with the tail of a fish, Capricorns are the practical and creative doers of the zodiac calendar. With the sure-footed hooves of the Goat, Capricorns can approach their goals with perseverance and authority, whilst their fishy tail suggests that they may also have a creative and sensitive side hiding beneath their stoic features. Earth sign Capricorns will usually find comfort in solid things and enjoy following a clear path that has tangible rewards at the end of it. This Goat isn't about taking the easy route, though, and Capricorns can be found confidently scaling the trickiest and longest paths with their stubbornly hardworking attitude. Born at the start of winter, the Goat is happy to take the path less trodden and seek out their own way in life, which can give them a reputation for being a loner to some extent. The Goat can be a serious soul thanks to their authoritative planet of Saturn, so would do well to try and lighten up from time to time and remember what it was like to be a kid again.

SATURN

The second largest planet in the solar system, Saturn rules over the eye-catching Capricorn. Dead set on achieving their goals, this groundbreaking earth sign is likely to be well known in whatever they choose to do in their lives. Named after the Roman god of agriculture, Saturn-led Capricorns can be wonderful at sowing a seed, working the earth and watching the abundant fruits of their labour grow to fruition. Despite Saturday being the namesake of Capricorn's ruling planet, this Saturn sign can struggle to say goodbye to their work and hello to the weekend. The planet of authority and discipline might not make Saturn an obvious choice for kicking off a fun-filled weekend, but it is a forced reminder that breaks must be taken and marks a tradition that even this sign can't ignore. For Capricorns, taking time away from their work can be tough so their ruling planet, Saturn, can act as an important reminder that all work and no play makes Capricorn as useful as a dull blade.

ELEMENTS, MODES AND POLARITIES

Each sign is made up of a unique combination of three defining groups: elements, modes and polarities. Each of these defining parts can manifest in good and bad ways, and none should be seen to be a positive or a negative — including the polarities! Just like a jigsaw puzzle, piecing these groups together can help illuminate why each sign has certain characteristics and help us find a balance.

ELEMENTS

Fire: Dynamic and adventurous, signs with fire in them can be extroverted. Others are naturally drawn to them because of the positive light they give off, as well as their high levels of energy and confidence.

Earth: Signs with the earth element are steady and driven with their ambitions. They make for a solid friend, parent or partner due to their grounded influence and nurturing nature.

Air: The invisible element that influences each of the other elements significantly, air signs will provide much-needed perspective to others with their fair thinking, verbal skills and key ideas.

Water: Warm in the shallows and sometimes freezing as ice, this mysterious element is essential to the growth of everything around it, through its emotional depth and empathy.

MODES

Cardinal: Pioneers of the calendar, cardinal signs jump-start each season and are the energetic go-getters.

Fixed: Marking the middle of the calendar, fixed signs firmly denote and value steadiness and reliability.

Mutable: As the seasons end, the mutable signs adapt and give themselves over gladly to the promise of change.

POLARITIES

Positive: Typically extroverted, positive signs take physical action and embrace outside stimulus in their life.

Negative: Usually introverted, negative signs value emotional development and experiencing life from the inside out.

CAPRICORN IN BRIEF

The table below shows the key attributes of Capricorn.
Use it for quick reference and to understand more about this fascinating sign.

SYMBOL	RULING PLANET	MODE	ELEMENT	HOUSE
The Sea Goat	Saturn	Cardinal	Earth	Tenth

COLOUR	BODY PARTS	POLARITY	GENDER	POLAR SIGN
Brown	Joints, Bones and Teeth	Negative	Feminine	Cancer

ROMANTIC RELATIONSHIPS

. . . .

Despite Capricorn's fishy tail suggesting a sensitive side seen in water signs, it's unlikely that this earth sign will feel all that comfortable with emotional displays of affection. When a Capricorn wants to express to their other half just how much they mean to them, it may be by way of physical gifts, like a box of expensive chocolates or even a new car. The greatest romantic gift for a Capricorn will usually be an engagement ring, as marriage will be essential to many of this sign, partly due to their desire for security and their value of upholding tradition. Giving a partner emotional support and stability can be essential in any relationship, but for the pragmatic Capricorn, who can be too focused on providing financial security for their loved ones, this can at times be forgotten. If a Capricorn is in the habit of showing their love by ways of expensive present-giving, they should remember that gifts of the greatest value do not always have the highest price tags.

Born in the tenth house in the zodiac calendar that focuses on careers and vocation, a Capricorn can be guilty of prioritising their work above their relationship. For a Capricorn, they may view the long hours that they are spending at the office as a sacrifice that they are happy to make for their partner in order to provide them with a beautiful home, money for holidays, or expensive cars. Whilst a Capricorn is unlikely to be deliberately neglecting their partner, usually being highly devoted in their relationships, establishing a balance between home life and work life can be essential to Capricorns finding long-term happiness in love. Finding a playful partner that can coax this Goat sign out from their desk of solitude and persuade them to relax and enjoy life is key for Capricorns in love.

ARIES: COMPATIBILITY 1/5

The cynical Capricorn is not an obvious lover for ambitious Aries but shouldn't necessarily be ruled out entirely as a potential partner. Capricorns usually take longer to make up their mind about a partner than the quick-working Aries, so Aries will need to exert some patience and work at Capricorn's slower pace if they want this challenging relationship to work. Like with any relationships, their differences can be their strengths. Be mindful of not wanting to change each other and learn how each can make the other a better, more well-rounded person.

TAURUS: COMPATIBILITY 3/5

Capricorn and Taurus in love are loyal and true to each other. These two earth signs value hard work and are driven by their need to enjoy the fruits of their labours. The home that these two could build together will likely be full of beautiful and expensive objects, with a couple of prized cars jewelling their garage. Whilst both will have dreams of marriage, Capricorn is the more traditional one and will probably approach the subject first. Taurus should try to inject joy and fun into the relationship to teach Capricorn to enjoy the lighter side of life.

GEMINI: COMPATIBILITY 1/5

This earth and air coupling between Capricorn and Gemini may be an unlikely match but awareness of their differences could help create a stronger bond. Capricorns appreciate the tangible: a good career and beautiful home, whilst Geminis love exciting ideas and the invisible workings of the mind. Whilst a Gemini's mutable element fits well with the cardinal aspect of Capricorn, what drives Capricorn may be at odds with the interests of Gemini. This polar opposite couple, Capricorn negative and Gemini positive, may struggle to find common ground but could stand to learn the most from one another.

CANCER: COMPATIBILITY 5/5

Opposites on the zodiac calendar, Capricorn and Cancer can experience a tenacious love. When water sign Cancer rains down on earth sign Capricorn, they can create a beautiful life together. Symbolised often with a fish's tail, the Sea Goat that represents Capricorn can swim happily in a Cancerian's warm waters. A Cancerian can indeed help coax a playfulness in Capricorn that others don't always see. Capricorns are ruled by the authoritative planet of Saturn, so could be a strong parenting partner for the family-orientated Cancerian. If these two hardworking signs fall in love with each other, the dedication that they share could be staggering.

LEO: COMPATIBILITY 4/5

Leo and Capricorn are the success story of opposites falling in love. Both these signs tend to have a clear sense of purpose; for Leo, it is in their personal life goals and for Capricorn, a clear career path is their focus. Leo Barack Obama and Capricorn Michelle Obama are an ideal example of how well these two can work towards achieving their dreams together. Capricorn can show Leo what hard work can accomplish, and Leo can bring the fun that sometimes the cool and dignified Capricorn can be lacking. Leo and Capricorn are two strong characters that can be even stronger together.

VIRGO: COMPATIBILITY 4/5

When the hardworking Capricorn and meticulous Virgo fall in love, there won't be many cracks in their relationship. With a Virgo's toolkit of organisation and practical skills and a Capricorn's portfolio of material achievements, this couple may be great at taking on exciting and grand projects together. Perhaps building their own home somewhere in the countryside would suit this couple, where their shared earth element can be appreciated at its best and their quieter negative energies embraced. This firm relationship may lack some spontaneity, so thoughtful surprises now and again could help keep their home fires burning.

LIBRA: COMPATIBILITY 1/5

The firm-footed Goat of Capricorn and high-spirited air sign of Libra could have little shared ground and struggle to strike a balance in love, but a relationship should not be ruled out. Born in the seventh house of relationships, Libras may struggle if Capricorns, born in the tenth house of careers, put their job before their partnership, so finding a middle ground between work and personal life will be essential for a happy union. It could be hard to find equality for this earth and air match when their differences are so vast, though their commitment could well outweigh any differences.

SCORPIO: COMPATIBILITY 5/5

When Capricorn and Scorpio set their sights on each other, these highly dedicated signs could be in it for the long run. Placed two apart on the zodiac calendar, theirs is a devout bond that is likely to be highly compatible with matching negative energies, complementary elements, and strong cardinal and fixed modes. A Capricorn can offer the security that Scorpio desires and Scorpio can be the powerful influence that feeds Capricorn's ambition. Scorpio will bring the fun and Capricorn will bring the itinerary to go with it. If they can take it in turns to rule the roost, their love could go the distance.

SAGITTARIUS: COMPATIBILITY 2/5

A materialist Capricorn and dazzling Sagittarius can both be guilty of feeling a little superior, which won't do in a partnership, especially when these two can have such different approaches to life. The rational Capricorn may be fearful of going to daring heights with their lively Sagittarius partner, but if they are open to Sagittarian's optimism, they could learn to love more bravely. A Sagittarius may feel constrained by Capricorn's constant reminder that actions have consequences, but looking before they leap could be a vital lesson that a Capricorn teaches their Sagittarian partner. The key to their happiness may be embracing each other's opposites.

CAPRICORN: COMPATIBILITY 3/5

Through better and through worse, there's probably no peak that these two Goats could not reach together. When a cardinal couple like two Capricorns fall in love, their accomplishments can be great. However, arguments over who is the driver in this partnership can cause rifts. Like any long journey or long-term relationship, it's all about taking turns behind the wheel; someone should remember to bring the car games as fun may be forgotten by this serious pair. Both earth signs, these two may be focused on material things, but they are also devoted and grounded partners to one another.

AQUARIUS: COMPATIBILITY 1/5

Both ruled by Saturn, Capricorns and Aquarians will usually have a good understanding of the rules of love. However, Aquarians are co-ruled by Uranus so may rebel against the traditions that most Capricorns value. A Capricorn and an Aquarius can both be extremely independent people, which may be what attracts them to one another, and as a creative couple they can really bring out the best in each other. This is a union of strong personalities and beliefs that may struggle to find common ground due to their opposite negative and positive energies, although their differences and determination could be their success.

PISCES: COMPATIBILITY 3/5

An earth and water love is bound to be a complementary match, and the relationship with a Capricorn and Piscean may be about helping each other grow as individuals and flourish as a couple. Capricorn will bring a practical mind and an active spirit with their cardinal nature, whilst the mutable Piscean will provide compassion and teach their Goat to be flexible. Both sides can retreat into themselves in times of great focus or reflection, particularly Pisceans if their Goat partner is being overbearing. However, their matching negative energies could form a deep emotional connection with each other and demonstrate true patience and dedication.

FAMILY AND FRIENDS

. . . .

Capricorns are the hard workers of the zodiac calendar, and a big driving force as to why they work so hard can be their family. A Capricorn may have ambitions of being the provider to their loved ones, providing food on the table, money for school trips, and a nice roof over their heads. Capricorns are usually house-proud individuals and for good reason, with their traditional taste and appreciation of materials, their house may have original beam features or luxurious sofas that show off their love for sturdy and tangible objects. Building a solid and secure home life for their family may be a Capricorn's dream and their self-sufficiency and drive can make them determined not to rely on others. Capricorns should be careful of becoming too focused on their work life and neglecting their home life as they might find that they start to alienate themselves from their loved ones if they do. Sharing responsibilities will free them up to enjoy the fruits of their labours and the real treasures in their life, which, for homebody Capricorn, is truly their family.

Like everything else in a Capricorn's life, friendships too may be measured by their value. For some cool kids, this cardinal Goat sign may seek out friendships that they believe will advance their social status further, as is their talent for sniffing out a solid investment. Whilst Capricorns love having control over their destiny, this sign would do well to leave the strategising in their financial lives and out of their friendships if they don't want to get a reputation of using people for their own personal gain. When Capricorns take a day off from planning their empires, they may find that the unexpected or oldest friendships this sign has are the most rewarding and worth investing more time in. Capricorns are a steady force of friendship, ready to support their loved ones through good times and bad. But they may not always be as receptive to help from their friends. Positive and high energy signs like Leo and Sagittarius can help Capricorns loosen up and learn to not just live life to its maximum, but to have fun whilst doing so, too.

As a child, parents can be the first and key figure of authority in most people's lives, but for Saturn-ruled Capricorn, their first experience of discipline and establishing boundaries can be even more relevant. Should a Capricorn have their own children, or look after other people's children, their Saturn influence will mean that their deep-set feelings of responsibility may make them a strict parent or guardian as they will not take these duties lightly. Setting curfews, dishing out chores and checking homework could be jobs that the Capricorn parent takes in their stride. Capricorns may also want to teach their child practical skills like learning to drive or riding a bike and will no doubt take huge pride in witnessing and being part of their children's achievements.

MONEY AND CAREERS

....

Being a certain star sign will not dictate the type of career that you have, although the characteristics that fall under each sign could help you identify the areas in which you could potentially thrive. Conversely, to succeed in the workplace, it is just as important to understand what you are good at as it is to know what you are less brilliant at, so that you can see the areas you need to work harder in to achieve your career and financial goals.

Belonging to the tenth house, where occupation and vocation are everything, it is no wonder that this sign has a great chance of rising up the ranks in their chosen profession. As a cardinal sign ruled by the authoritative planet of Saturn, Capricorns can suit high-powered and high-earning jobs, such as a director or CEO of a company. Ambition is Capricorn's middle name and thanks to their cardinal nature, their drive for success can see them become trailblazers in their professional field. Trendsetting designer Diane von Fürstenberg, activist leader Martin Luther King Jr. and pioneer of glam rock David Bowie are all Capricorns who have lit the way for others to follow by climbing their personal ladders to success. Whatever this Sea Goat sets their mind to, Capricorn's tenacity, teamed with their strong will, means that whilst they may take a while getting wherever they are going, their destination will be worth it. They will not be afraid of being different, nor will they apologise for forging new paths. Capricorns know who they are and where they want to be, so work hard to achieve their goals.

Capricorns are one of the earth signs of the zodiac, so tangible objects can bring this sign great satisfaction. Certificates, trophies and medals will usually adorn Capricorns' walls, shelves and neck, as a visual reminder of the greatness that they can achieve. Careers where a Capricorn can use their practical skills, perhaps as a property developer or learning a specific trade, may suit this sign as it could satisfy their need for material things and provide them with a solid outcome and income from their hard work. Capricorns are usually careful with money, apart from when they are trying to impress someone, in which cases they may be caught spending beyond their means in order to try and make a good impression. Whilst Capricorns may be seen to splurge, any expenses that this sign makes will be judged on what they will receive in return, so a Capricorn will probably view their spending more as investing. The returns may not always be monetary, but Capricorns will value appreciation of their gifts.

Whilst you can't always choose who you work with, it can be advantageous to learn about colleagues' key characteristics through their star signs to try and work out the best ways of working with them. Like Capricorns, Virgos can be wonderful planners, so these to-do list lovers could very well be responsible for overseeing the Christmas work do or co-presenting at important meetings together, managing projects with precision and panache. Taureans can work doggedly with hard-working Capricorns through the most difficult of tasks, and will bond over their shared grit and determination to see tasks through to the end even if the odds seem to be against them. Capricorn's cardinal nature can mean that they are happy to work on their own and may clash with other cardinal signs in a contest for power. However, inspiring Aries and passionate Cancerians can make for stimulating cardinal colleagues.

HEALTH AND WELLBEING

· · · · · · · · · · · · · · · · ·

When you are as adept at climbing so many ladders in life, overcoming obstacles and conquering mountains like the Goat in Capricorn is, you may also find that you have the legs for great physical challenges. Running marathons, cycling on rocky terrains or mountaineering could all be challenges the sporty Capricorn enjoys. If there is a shiny medal or trophy to be won at the end of it, then all the better for this magpie sign. Associated with joints and bones, Capricorns may like to pay extra attention to looking after these areas of the body. So, once this mountain Goat has picked up their medals for their sporting achievements, taking the time to unwind with some yoga stretches will no doubt help keep their tired joints from seizing up on them. Eating a balanced diet rich in omega-3 from plenty of fish and nuts could help keep joints loose and well-oiled whilst taking relevant supplements could also put the pep back into a Capricorn's step.

Capricorns can be oh-so serious, worrying about this or that and planning everything within an inch of its life so that they achieve the staggering excellence that they are after. But striving for success, whilst being a motivational force, can at times be a tough burden to bear, particularly if a Capricorn's dreams aren't going to plan. This sign can have a reputation for being pessimistic in their pragmatic approach to life, and their grumbling can lead to moaning which can leave them with a cold and hard view of the world. Indeed, when life gives Capricorn lemons, the severe disappointment that they are left with can make it hard to see how exactly they can make lemonade. For a sign that likes to feel sure-footed, not knowing where they stand can rattle this sign and leave them feeling unsteady and uneasy. Control might not be an easy thing for Capricorns to let go of, but the sooner this sign accepts that certain things cannot be predicted, the sooner they can relax and enjoy the unknown.

Keeping Capricorn's health and wellbeing in check may be linked to keeping their work and personal life balanced. Too often, a Capricorn can put their work duties ahead of their health and happiness by working themselves to the bone on a regular basis. A Capricorn may feel better initially by staying late in the office or answering work emails at the weekend as a way of staying on top of their heavy workloads, however, working endlessly is not sustainable for any sign and a burnout could be just around the corner if this sign is not careful. Capricorns' work ethics can be admirable, but they can be so fixed on their end goal that they may not see that the journey is damaging their health and wellbeing. The key for Capricorns may be to rest just as hard as they work, as all work and no downtime is never good for any sign.

Capricorn

· · · · · · · · · · · · · · ·

DAILY FORECASTS
for 2021

OCTOBER
. . . .

Friday 1st

Get ready for a weekend of connections and deep intimacy, but you must always remember to be respectful of other's boundaries. Today, you have the right amount of curiosity, energy and courage to take steps that you deemed too big for you in the past. Be adventurous and explore life's mysteries.

Saturday 2nd

Be good and take smaller steps if you notice that you're triggering someone. It can be challenging today as you may be invited into a confidence, but not know where the borders are. Amorous Venus may help you loosen up a little today.

Sunday 3rd

Mercury retrograde connects to Jupiter, making any mishaps much larger and possibly off the scale. Tread carefully around work issues and always aim for balance and understanding. Read between the lines in conversations. This is also a good day to detox, declutter or do something else that is good for your body.

Monday 4th

You may be torn between short-term and long-term goals today. What satisfies you now isn't usual for you, and you are aware of this. Inspiration from your travel and higher education sector may provide you with a new artistic or romantic pursuit. Others will be pleasantly surprised.

Tuesday 5th

Today you may have to be strict about how much you give to others. Your time may be in demand, but you must look after number one. You should consider letting go of things that are no longer good for you, including bad habits, coping mechanisms and outdated thinking.

Wednesday 6th

A new moon in your career sector allows you to set goals and intentions around your work and aspirations. This moon also contacts Mars and Mercury; this is a great day to ask for a rise or to get a review. Pluto turns direct, too. Feel the pressure lift from your sector of self.

Thursday 7th

Venus enters your hidden sector now, where she will entice you to do more introspection and self-care. You may feel this intensely and react with anticipation and defensiveness. Feel your way into it, but ensure that you allow yourself plenty of alone time now, even if just to spoil yourself.

Friday 8th

The Sun and Mars meet and make a powerhouse of great energy in your career sector. Projects will likely steam ahead and be successful now. Be careful today, as someone in your social circle may upset you. There may be a nasty edge to this person.

Saturday 9th

Today is all about communications. Mercury is in the heart of the Sun and receiving new information. Your job is to listen and not speak. He's sitting with Mars, so you may feel restless and find it almost impossible not to say anything. Keep your mouth zipped.

Sunday 10th

Saturn, your ruler, goes direct today. This is good news, as you will now feel more forward motion regarding finances and value. Spend some time alone and readjust your thoughts. A weight has been lifted and you have been given the green light. Try to pick up on clues and messages from Mercury.

Monday 11th

Your private time will benefit from a little detective work today. There could be something that has been hidden from you, but is now coming to the surface. A search for truth and justice may begin to yield results. You might wish to break free from old habitual patterns.

Tuesday 12th

This is a quiet day, so you might decide to pick up your artistic endeavours and get creative. Cooking exotic dishes or adding sensuous furnishings to your home can help you feel grounded. The Moon is in your sign and you may like to treat yourself now. And why not?

Wednesday 13th

Newly direct Pluto greets the Moon and you notice what has left your life in the past few months. This may not be something you wished for, but Pluto, who deals with permanent endings, has done it for you. Is there space for something new and exciting to come in?

Thursday 14th

Saturn is your teacher today and you may find that you're reviewing issues around money, social groups and rebelliousness. Have you learned anything from Saturn's retrograde? You are often too strict on yourself; now is the time to loosen the reins a little. Splash out on something nice.

Friday 15th

You may see some issues with bosses or people in authority today. Jupiter hosts the Moon and expands any mood you're currently feeling. It is likely that you over-inflate your own ego and get uptight. Take a deep breath and be humble, as you possibly need to apologise now.

Saturday 16th

Today you are more forgiving and can go with the flow more easily. You may be talking to those who inspire you to dream or get spiritual. Short visits can be a labour of love or a quest to an end goal. Pause and reflect before making any definitive choices.

Sunday 17th

Jupiter turns direct today. That is another heavyweight shifted from your finances and value sector. Take some time to realign yourself as the Moon meets Neptune. You may see something worth pursuing, even though Neptune is still retrograde.

Monday 18th

Mercury joins the others and turns direct, giving you some breathing space in the workplace. You may need to go over the events of the last three weeks and look at where Mercury has called for a review, a redo or a recall. Now you have the chance to put it all right.

Tuesday 19th

You may be action-orientated today, and eager to get on and do the things that the retrogrades have somehow prevented you doing. Take small steps and don't rush to do everything all at once. It's possible that you're bombarded with instructions or messages to deal with today.

Wednesday 20th

Today, there's a full moon in your family sector. How many of your plans from the last six months have come to fruition? Celebrate those that have and don't mourn the ones that haven't. You may feel momentarily tired, exhausted even, but if you rest, you will soon be back on your feet.

Thursday 21st

Restless energy fills you up and you have the urge to dance, rebel or do something artistic. Some of the ideas you have today will be too radical or unconventional, so look to what is sensible. Use this energy to produce something beautiful or to speak words of love.

Friday 22nd

Mars and Pluto are squaring off today and you may see a few power struggles surfacing. This could be at work, where your status is challenged. However, if you can look at things slightly differently, there should be a happy outcome for everyone involved.

Saturday 23rd

The Sun enters your social sector now. It's possible that your interest groups widen and the topics you choose to share become more obscure or taboo. You may look at the darker side of life and get involved with people who have esoteric knowledge. This may be a very secretive time.

Sunday 24th

Today is one of those days where you run around doing a lot of things for other people and have no time for yourself. You may have a list of chores to get through and only find rest at bedtime. Ensure that you don't get exhausted by taking short breaks throughout the day.

Monday 25th

Your dreams and visions seem far away. You're likely to question whether they are all just a mirage. Plan to share time with a lover or special person this evening. Your need to be nurtured, if only for a short while, may surface tonight. Let yourself be looked after.

Tuesday 26th

If you can possibly let yourself relax and be cared for today, you may receive a pleasant surprise. Your head and heart are not in agreement, so don't try reconciling them. Have a dreamy day with someone who cares for you. Messages of support and encouragement will satisfy you.

Wednesday 27th

You may have had enough of being nurtured now and hit the limit of your patience. You might struggle to break free, but you must remember to be kind and give gratitude to others. Venus is asking that you come back to yourself and process things alone.

Thursday 28th

It's likely that you lack energy today and sink deeper into dependency on someone special. You will find this difficult and feel as though you have let yourself down. Turn towards spiritual practices when you need to feel connected, as you might find people too much for you at these times.

Friday 29th

Today you may be too bold and outspoken for your own good.
You're possibly boastful or obnoxious. Mercury connects to
the Moon, giving you the power of speech, but it may not go
the way you wish it to. Back off or erupt, it's your choice.

Saturday 30th

Mars enters your social sector. Expect there to be some heated
discussions. Things are already quite tense in your friendship
groups and you may see some splits or witness friendships
dissolve. This evening, you want to analyse what happened.
Was there something you missed?

Sunday 31st

The Moon and Sun make a helpful connection for you to do
some detective work. You may be scrutinising recent events
and looking at every detail. It's possible that you unearth
something that may be seen as radical, but in a good way.
You seek truth and justice, and you may just get that.

NOVEMBER

· · · · · · · · · · · · · · · · ·

Monday 1st

Mercury and Jupiter combine to make your words count today.
It's possible that you're standing up for the underdog at work
or stating your own case. Either way, this will go well for you.
Money matters may be raised, so be sure to check out your
bank balance and work budgets.

Tuesday 2nd

A harmonising moon in your careers sector makes a helpful
connection to Saturn, the teacher planet. As he's your ruler,
there will be something you must pay attention to and take
on board. Bosses, elders or other leaders will be involved.
Control what you say or there may be trouble.

Wednesday 3rd

The Moon meets Mercury today. There's something on your
mind and you feel so passionate about it that you need to get
it off your chest. However, wait for the right time to speak up.

Thursday 4th

After meeting Mars, the aggressive planet, the Moon becomes
new in your social sector. This can be a tricky time, where you
realise the need to make changes or end certain friendships
that have become volatile or stale. Venus urges you to put
yourself first and release some stress.

Friday 5th

Venus enters your sign. She will ensure that you are hard-working but remain kind to yourself. Mercury enters your social sector. There will be a tendency to gossip now, and some rumours may be spread. Stay away if you aren't directly involved as things could get nasty.

Saturday 6th

You may be attempting to mediate between friends or other social groups. Alternatively, you may be fighting for your place in the group. You have a lot of processing to do before you fully understand this situation. Now isn't the time to act. Be responsible and respectful, always.

Sunday 7th

It will be difficult to see another point of view today, even if you try. Thoughts may be affecting your routine as you can't still your mind. You are feeling self-righteous or indignant, but the truth will come out if you're patient.

Monday 8th

The Moon meets Venus in your sign. Indulge yourself with this soft feminine energy and look at ways to self-soothe. Your reputation is important to you and you are defending it strongly. Today, you may see a difference or a shift in the way you're perceived.

Tuesday 9th

Maybe it's time to let someone or something go now.
You've worked hard for long enough, but have you seen the
results you desire? Neptune draws you back to your inner
compass. If something doesn't feel right, then it isn't in
alignment and you must transform or discard it.

Wednesday 10th

This is an unfavourable day for some friendship groups.
There may be a feeling of the group coming together for a
common purpose, but look deeper. People may have their
own agendas and some are at odds. Harsh words may be
spoken when Mars and Mercury meet.

Thursday 11th

If a negative situation has come to a head, there may be
unexpected results. If you want to raise a revolution, then
this is the day to do it. Otherwise, get out of the crowd and
don't get involved.

Friday 12th

Your true north is in sight today, so grab it with both hands.
This may be your saving grace. Take a different approach to
achieve your goals. You may have realised recently that you
have been climbing the wrong mountain. Take some time out
for a solitary practice such as meditation.

Saturday 13th

Mercury opposes Uranus, so there's still the possibility of upset or spiteful words between friends. However, this can be softened when the Moon meets Neptune, as you have the chance to see another side to things. You may also be strict and dispose of what is not serving you now.

Sunday 14th

What you want and what you feel are in sync today, and this helps you to put plans into action. Family may be supportive or need encouragement from you to get things going. It's up to you to make the change you need in your life right now.

Monday 15th

You may have a little setback today and discover that there is more work to be done than you first thought. Your social groups are coming back into order. Take your responsibilities seriously and make plans to give yourself more downtime.

Tuesday 16th

You are on top form and doing what it takes to make a permanent change. However, this may leave you feeling drained and exhausted by the end of the day, so be sure to factor in some time to rest or switch off before bedtime.

Wednesday 17th

Today, you seek solace in your artistic pursuits. Mars sits opposite Uranus and this restless, volatile energy needs to create something. If you have no projects in mind, a good home-cooked meal with special friends will suffice. You may also wish to move your body with some exercise.

Thursday 18th

The Moon meets Uranus and you could feel conflicted. Where did your energy go? Mercury fills your head with nonsense and Neptune draws you to dream impossible dreams. This will soon pass, so go with the flow and see where it takes you today.

Friday 19th

The build-up to the full moon today has been intense and may have knocked you from your centre. The best thing you can do is to ground yourself with practical earthy activities. Look at what you have created in the last six months and celebrate your successes and achievements.

Saturday 20th

You may feel that you need a quiet weekend. Stick to your mundane duties and obligations and gently work through your list of chores. There may be a choice of things at the end of the day to help you relax. Some casual chat with friends or siblings will while away the hours.

Sunday 21st

You are commended on your sense of duty today. Take pride in the way you ensure that the people important to you have all they need and are OK. Calling on elders in the family will be gratifying for both you and them. Think rationally and logically now.

Monday 22nd

The Moon has shifted into your relationship sector and you may choose to spend time with a partner or close friend. Venus and Mars support any romantic connections you have today. The Sun has entered your hidden sector. What dark corners will it shine on to be healed?

Tuesday 23rd

You'll need to let someone take the lead today. This may unsettle you as you're a natural leader, but will let you have some breathing space. The energy is emotional and fluid, so spend time feeling, relating and connecting on a level that is not that familiar to you.

Wednesday 24th

Mercury joins the Sun in your hidden sector. Listen to your dreams, as there may be important messages and clues there for you. You break away from connecting with a loved one and may have learned how to do this without causing upset. It's time for your voice to be heard.

Thursday 25th

Mars and Venus are connecting well, making relating to
another person easy. The Moon is in your intimacy sector
and you can speak your truth without fear. This is a good
day for romance if you're respectful of personal boundaries.

Friday 26th

You may look at what's important to you now. It's possible that
this has changed over the course of the year. Group ventures
may not be as good as you first thought. Insist on speaking
your mind, but do so with compassion. Truth and justice have
come to mean more to you than they once did.

Saturday 27th

It may be time for a declutter or detox. If you are studying, you
might wish to go through your notes, as you'll see more details
and omissions now. Your mind and heart are not in sync, so time
is better spent alone. Take a pause to get your cluttered mind
into a place where you feel it needs to be.

Sunday 28th

Stay in the mindset of being methodical and you may see that
your workload decreases. This is you being more efficient and
giving your attention to practical, honest work. External dramas
can be too distracting for you. Get the job done today with
no daydreaming.

Monday 29th

Once again, Mercury is in the heart of the Sun. If you're observant, you may notice subtle messages or hints enter your awareness. This is Mercury's way of telling you what he has found in your psyche and what needs to come up for healing. Note this for a later date.

Tuesday 30th

Your ruler, Saturn, is connecting to the Sun and Mercury. This means that your next lesson may be hard work, but ultimately essential to your self-development. You have a little time to dream today; Venus and Neptune let you realign with your inner compass and you feel satisfied with your progress.

DECEMBER

· · · · · · · · · · · · · · · · · · ·

Wednesday 1st

Finishing up work projects is possible this morning, with the Moon in your career sector. Tie up loose ends and make sure that everyone is on the same page. This afternoon, Neptune finally turns direct and you will now be able to make some great forward shifts to get closer to your true north.

Thursday 2nd

This is a great day to come to terms with anything that is intense or difficult for you to process. When you do your best, you will be perceived well by others. This may be challenging if you resist authority and can cause conflict, so play by the rules.

Friday 3rd

The Moon meets Mars in your social sector. This can have the effect of getting your friends together for a vigorous activity, but could also mean that aggression or tempers are likely. You may come up against a big character who likes to throw their weight around. Keep your temper under control.

Saturday 4th

There is a new moon in your hidden sector today. Spending time alone and making a personal agenda for the coming year will help you form new plans. You may like to spread your wings a bit more. Listen to what Mercury has to say when he meets the Moon. Think logically and rationally.

Sunday 5th

The Moon makes a great connection to Jupiter, who tells you to think big. Whatever you secretly desire for your self-improvement will be enhanced. There is also the possibility of enjoying your alone time so much that you stay in solitude a little longer than normal. This won't do you any harm.

Monday 6th

Mars in your social sector connects to Pluto. These two together can bring sudden change or events that are spontaneous and unexpected. It's possible that a friendship will end, or you disconnect from a group that has proved disappointing. Tune in to your own needs and wants, and get back on course.

Tuesday 7th

The Moon meets Pluto in your sign and you may get confirmation that something has outlived its usefulness to you. You may grieve the loss of this, but remain hopeful that you have done the right thing. You must stick to your guns and not back down.

Wednesday 8th

Today may be difficult, as the planetary energy is restless and restrictive. Trouble is stirred up easily. Someone in your social circle might make a scene that involves more people than is needed. You may have a brush with the law or need professional help in some way.

Thursday 9th

Look at your finances today. The upset in your social sector
may have drained your resources. Your wider interest groups
might also be affected. Take time to get your thoughts together
before reprimanding someone. This afternoon, you should feel
more connected to the collective.

Friday 10th

Give yourself a break today and dispose of some of your
restless energy. Speak your mind by all means, but find a way
of doing so that is respectful. You may wish to write things
down and present an idea, a concept or a letter of complaint.

Saturday 11th

Venus meets Pluto today. This can be seen as manipulation,
passive-aggression or power struggles. Watch out for this and
stay alert. The Moon meets newly direct Neptune. If you get
sight of your dreams, hold onto them and start making plans
to manifest them. Your self-talk can be overwhelming today.

Sunday 12th

The Moon is now in your family sector. You may need to
get active and take a role in the upcoming festivities. Get
your planner out and schedule the weeks ahead with your
tribe. Venus is still with Pluto, so be mindful that you could
potentially get coaxed into doing something.

Monday 13th

Mars marches into your hidden sector and will not stay still.
You may have some restless nights while he's here. Likewise,
Mercury enters your sign. Your powers of communication will
be on top form now. You're likely to experience a few weeks of
racing thoughts with these two shifts.

Tuesday 14th

Get creative or productive today. You may have a need to
treat yourself or buy in some good foods for the holiday
season. There's a chance that you overspend. If you do, you
will probably need to justify this to yourself at a later date,
so be sensible.

Wednesday 15th

Have you bent the rules today? The Moon sits with Uranus and
you're feeling rebellious. A person in authority is watching and
isn't impressed. Perhaps your own self-indulgence has got the
better of you. Is that luxury purchase really necessary?
Think twice before being impulsive.

Thursday 16th

You'll possibly find yourself feeling more positive today.
The control issues may have turned around to your advantage.
It's likely that you have made the first step towards claiming
your true north and feel good about this. Don't worry if you
have upset someone in the process, they'll get over it.

Friday 17th

As the weekend approaches, you'll probably feel that your
list of chores is endless. There may be a lot to prepare for the
festive season and you find yourself running around. This
could trigger you to want to be alone and do your own thing,
but this isn't possible right now. Is there something you can
do for yourself without neglecting your other duties?

Saturday 18th

If you feel as if you have already lost sight of your dreams,
remember that the bigger life is pretty busy at this time and
you simply need to go with the flow. There will be time for
your dream plans later. Work through your to-do list today.

Sunday 19th

Venus turns retrograde in your sign. You may have issues
around love or maintaining harmony now. It's possible that
an old lover makes a reappearance. A full moon in your
health and duties sector could highlight a troublesome health
problem, or else show you where you do too much for others.

Monday 20th

You turn to a close friend or lover for some peace today.
Your heart and head are at odds, and you may say something
out of the blue. Soothing company and good food will take
your mind off things. Allow yourself to be nurtured until you
feel ready to face the world again.

Tuesday 21st

The winter solstice arrives. Today is best spent being cosy with
a loved one. The Sun enters your sign as if to agree with this.
This longest night may have you contemplating the year gone
by and sharing thoughts and dreams with a lover or close friend.

Wednesday 22nd

The courageous Moon in your intimacy sector is getting
you ready for the celebrations. You may be stepping out
and partying already. You want to say what is on your mind,
regardless of the consequences. Be mindful that you don't
upset someone you care a lot for. Don't be too impulsive.

Thursday 23rd

Jupiter is at the end of your finance and value sector. This is
a critical time and you might just blow the bank. Be careful
with your spending, as Jupiter can exaggerate everything.
Your indulgent side may go overboard today.

Friday 24th

You have a need to check that everything is ready for the
big celebrations. This can be a day filled with tension and
arguments, as you might expect. The planets are not being
very helpful. Everyone has their own agenda, so try to come
to some sort of agreement with your nearest and dearest.

Saturday 25th

However you celebrate, be respectful and kind to those sharing your day. There is a tendency to take over or dominate, as Venus has met Pluto again. Put your own dreams aside and do your bit. Uranus and Mercury connect and herald a day of surprises and pleasant communication.

Sunday 26th

You may have reconnected with a person who is sympathetic to your vision for self-improvement. It's likely that you are discussing this in great detail today. You're in total control of what you want and know how you're going to go about getting it. Good for you.

Monday 27th

Today may be a little more peaceful, and allow you time to be quiet and listen to your thoughts. Someone may have recently given you food for thought. Your mood may be a nice balance of satisfaction and anticipation. Give respect where it's due and listen to your elders.

Tuesday 28th

Make sure that you're not coming across as a control freak. Your mouth might run away with you today and you could become a bossy boots. No one will thank you for this right now. Watch your ego, as it's likely to become over-inflated today. This will not do you any favours.

Wednesday 29th

Jupiter finally returns to your communication sector. He will stay here for the next twelve months, so think big, plan big and stretch your boundaries now. Your energy is sociable but pushy today. You may breach a personal boundary and upset someone close. There is a sting in your words.

Thursday 30th

Mercury meets Pluto today. If you can't say something nice, you're better off saying nothing. Mercury will accept his new mission for you, so look out for signs. The secretive, intense moon in your social sector is emotionally attached to this. This is about self-respect, self-control and owning your power.

Friday 31st

The end of the year is here and you find yourself evaluating the year gone by. The Moon sits with Mars in your hidden sector. You may be wound up or anxious. Get out and join in the fun. Be a party animal tonight.

Capricorn

....

DAILY FORECASTS
for 2022

JANUARY

· · · · · · · · · · · · · · · · · ·

Saturday 1st

Happy New Year and welcome to 2022. You begin the year
feeling extremely positive and full of ideas. You may need to
take a realistic look at what will be achievable for your usual
steady mode of climbing personal mountains. Get creative
and expressive. People will notice.

Sunday 2nd

There is a new moon in your sign today. What goals and
intentions would you like to set now? This is a great way to
start the year. You may find that unusual pursuits attract you
now. Get your thinking cap on as radical approaches to old
problems may come into your awareness.

Monday 3rd

Old loves may make an appearance. This will take up space in
your emotions today. If these appear as wounds that still hurt,
do something that you enjoy and nurture yourself. Don't let
negativity consume you.

Tuesday 4th

You aren't one to dwell on emotions and would rather be
productive, but you may find that work doesn't flow easily.
There might be some problem-solving to do or hurdles to
climb over first. It's possible that you feel conflicted and
need to make rational decisions.

Wednesday 5th

If you can spend some time alone today, you will notice how driven your innermost thoughts are. You may be swimming in your own deepest psyche and pulling up old thought patterns and habits. Get inspired to change what no longer suits you. Your sense of injustice will kick in and you might find that you wallow over past hurts.

Thursday 6th

This could be a year when you improve on your finances. You may have some radical ideas about how to do this, so go with them. Only you know the dedication it takes to make dreams a reality. If there is something you have been wanting to do for a long time, act now.

Friday 7th

Your inner compass gives you a nudge in the right direction today, so pay attention. This may mean making short trips or a little research to take that critical first step. If you are the least bit emotionally invested in this, it can mean positive changes are on the way.

Saturday 8th

Family matters might consume your weekend and be fun. There may be a lot of chatter, gossip or plans being made. Others are in the mood to listen to uplifting plans, so let them hear yours. It may be that you meet someone who can be influential for you now.

Sunday 9th

Today may be a little difficult as your own needs and those of others clash. It's possible that you experience control issues. Ensure that your personal boundaries are strong, and you can keep yourself away from people who may drain your energy. Take time out if needed.

Monday 10th

Tension adds a bad taste to your day. You may be inclined to dig your heels in and be stubborn about something you have been asked to do. Be patient and ride this energy out as it will soon pass. Do some vigorous exercise or treat yourself to take your mind off it.

Tuesday 11th

Today you want your own way. Throwing a toddler tantrum will not help. You may need to toe the line and be humble. Bide your time until the time is right to put forward your own agenda. Try to see another perspective on this.

Wednesday 12th

Your sense of calm returns and you can concentrate on bigger matters. Important relationships may benefit from this today. You may be shown how difficult you have been, and an apology could be in order. Treat a loved one or person you admire to your better side now.

Thursday 13th

Use today to back up all your devices, double-check travel plans and ensure clear communication. The trickster planet Mercury will retrograde and may cause some problems with plans you share with large groups. Keep calm.

Friday 14th

You may already feel unsettled and dissatisfied with finances and home comforts. If you must be radical now, try changing something that can easily be restored if you don't like it. A home makeover or some new bedtime reading may shift those urges to switch things around.

Saturday 15th

Spend time today doing what makes you feel safe and protected. This may be time spent with a loved one, or in the company of maternal figures and home-cooked foods. You may find an internal itch that is asking to be scratched. Don't open old wounds today; nurture your inner child instead.

Sunday 16th

Tricky energy could mean that you blurt out a secret or say something you shouldn't. Even though it may come from the heart and be the instigator of much-needed change, it could still hurt someone. There might still be an old love from the past hanging around and stirring things up. Take care.

Monday 17th

Today's full moon in your opposite sign might see important relationships go under the spotlight. You may be more selfish now and disregard the feelings of others. You have your sights set on your future goals and they may not include the people who care about you.

Tuesday 18th

Take some time today to take stock of recent events. You may have a change of heart and wish to put things right. However, there is unstable energy around, and your best bet would be to lie low and do some deep thinking. Not everyone is as quick to make amends as you are.

Wednesday 19th

You might feel blocked and restricted today. You still want to speak your mind about what is important to you, but it will not go down well if you do. Use that restless energy in another way. Put pen to paper and write down your feelings or organise your thoughts.

Thursday 20th

Introspection about your own conditioned behaviour will help you today. You have the energy to dig deep and forge ahead with understanding your motives. You have a desire to learn more about things that are foreign to you, including how to serve your wider community. Be selfless today.

Friday 21st

Your restlessness may be appeased today by doing something creative. This could include a love interest and may be worth exploring further. Your unique ways of looking at the world may be appreciated by a person you are trying to impress. Sweetness and light work well for you today.

Saturday 22nd

Be careful that you are not seeing a situation or a person through rose-tinted glasses. It's possible that you are bewitched by flattering messages. This evening you become more balanced and begin to see through thin exteriors and into the reality of events. Keep it real.

Sunday 23rd

It's a 'now or never' day and you must stay alert to any hidden messages you may receive. These might come from within. You could have shadow material surface to be healed now. Staying home and taking care of your own needs is important.

Monday 24th

A light bulb turns on for you today and you have the exact amount of energy and motivation to start climbing your personal mountain this year. Get prepared. Check the road map and gather your resources. This may involve a bold career move and will bring big changes. Do not resist.

Tuesday 25th

Check in with your wider interest groups today as you may learn something useful. You have an intense need to turn to trusted friends for advice. Be mindful that conversations may not have as much clarity as you need right now, so keep it light and non-judgemental.

Wednesday 26th

You may feel blocked today as things are not happening as fast as you would like. There are two planets in retrograde in your sign now, so go easy on yourself. There may be tension in your love life and harsh words may be spoken, but at least this will shift things in a fresh direction for you.

Thursday 27th

The weekend is in sight and you desire to have some downtime. You can't move forward on anything just yet, so use this time for planning and adjusting. Old feelings of injustice may surface briefly, so deal with them as they come up.

Friday 28th

Elders in your wider community will have something to share with you today. This may go against your current way of thinking, but will be useful and worth listening to. Your inner compass is not working, and this is your cue to sit and listen to others who can teach you a lesson.

Saturday 29th

Today you may have some insight into your next mountain-climbing mission. Listen carefully as this is a new and improved version of the one you have now. You end the day with your motivation on top form. Grab your backpack and start climbing. You may surprise a loved one.

Sunday 30th

Your heart is full of love for your own projects. Self-care and gut instincts will guide you. A revolution is starting within. It may not be quite what you expected but it fires you up to act and follow your passions. Put your best foot forward.

Monday 31st

A moment of crisis keeps you awake and you may begin to doubt yourself. Take a good look at how this process has manifested so far this month and give yourself some credit. Go to friends and acquaintances, who are your cheerleaders, for words of encouragement. They will spur you onwards.

FEBRUARY

. . . .

Tuesday 1st

The new moon today is a chance to set goals and intentions
based on building your finances, connecting to groups
of people and learning about what you value. You have a
rebellious streak that needs directing in a way that builds
your empire and self-esteem. Learn to respect rules.

Wednesday 2nd

You may feel a little uneasy today and find yourself looking
back at what you have lost. There is much to gain now, so
look ahead instead. You may learn something by using your
emotional faculties to merge with others today. This could
fire up a passion you never knew you had.

Thursday 3rd

Today you are optimistic and fly through the day. Others
perceive a different side to you as you are caring, sharing and
ready to take on the world. You may have more empathy for
work colleagues and people you see every day. This will be
noticed by others.

Friday 4th

Mercury turns direct today in your sign. You may now get
back to the business of putting plans in place. Professional
development could be highlighted. Your inner compass is
working again and you approach the day with all guns blazing.
A high level of motivation moves you towards your goals.

Saturday 5th

Try not to neglect a loved one this weekend. You may have your sights set on your mountain and forget the other parts of your life. Enjoy some free time and learn to relax. Work will still be there when you return. Of course, this may mean that you neglect your own needs, too, so be mindful of that.

Sunday 6th

Your head and heart are not in sync today. You have many ideas and plans, but you have possibly already run out of steam. If you don't take time to rest and contemplate, you could be climbing up the wrong mountain. Don't take on more than you can manage.

Monday 7th

Today you are more inclined to ground your ideas and make them achievable. You may use your energy wisely and come up with unique ways of satisfying your urges. This may feel like a U-turn, but is, in fact, a more realistic and wholesome direction.

Tuesday 8th

Authority figures and egos may clash with your personal needs today. You might be called to justify yourself in some way. These blockages will soon pass. You have the power of persuasion and others may begin to see your point of view. Hold on to your inner compass and look to your true north.

Wednesday 9th

This is a good day to share your views with the outside world. You may find that you can be of service now simply by communicating with others. Pay attention to your health as all this thinking and strategising may be giving you tension headaches. Boost your immune system, too.

Thursday 10th

Just as you are thinking that you must be crazy, you get a boost of confidence from someone who can teach you great things. Look out for an important lesson today. It may look unnecessarily harsh, but will ultimately benefit your endeavours. Take note of who brings this lesson.

Friday 11th

A crucial moment of understanding may occur today. Something fits nicely into place and you seem to just know what to do. This could be a complete change of tactics that you hadn't considered before. Prepare to let an old way of thinking go and to embrace what a new one can teach you.

Saturday 12th

You know what you want and exactly how to get it now. Your desires and drive are perfectly in sync and will be for several weeks. You are fun to be around today as your optimism is addictive. Partners and intimate relationships benefit from this.

Sunday 13th

Be very careful not to tangle up your emotional support for someone close with meeting your own needs. You may need to separate the two today and understand that they are not the same thing. Your relationship with another and with yourself has different agendas. Make time for both.

Monday 14th

A realisation that you are being pulled out of alignment may make you resentful. Look carefully to see if you have been drifting before you point the finger. This may simply be a time to put yourself first. Something is about to shift, whether you like it or not.

Tuesday 15th

Pay attention to what you do to nurture yourself. This may be being productive but could also be something as simple as listening to music, reading a good book or chatting unconditionally with friends. Your inner lover may be stroking your ego and telling you to stop being too hard on yourself.

Wednesday 16th

There is a full moon today, which will highlight shared finances and the deeper mysteries of life. Do what makes you feel safe and protected now. Recognise that your own sense of worth is paramount to all that you do. If you believe you can do something, then you will.

Thursday 17th

Stop beating yourself up for taking care of your own needs. Remember that you can't pour from a cup that is empty, so fill your own cup first. You may be beginning to see that even a mountain goat needs nourishment. You might be inspired to learn something new.

Friday 18th

The balance is restored as you relax back into yourself and have energy for others. You don't worry about being on your true path as closeness and community are more important. Spending time with others is not so bad. You notice that small changes make big differences.

Saturday 19th

It's possible that you have a mind full of work at the weekend. However, if you stay mindful to your own needs, this can bring about a healthy balance of work and play for you. You may like to brainstorm some ideas with your wider groups or online community.

Sunday 20th

Just like a hardworking Capricorn, you have fallen back into a work-first mode. You will notice that your energy and drive are depleted once more, or that you are being accused of neglecting a loved one in favour of your own agenda. This is a lesson you need to review.

Monday 21st

Today you may seek the attention of a few trusted friends. There may be a hint of jealousy or secrecy in the air and you want to know about it. Don't be tempted to gossip. Be mindful that your desire and drive are still in sync and need satisfying.

Tuesday 22nd

There is intense energy around now and it may make you feel selfish or, at worst, hedonistic. There is no need to go to extremes today in anything you do. By evening, you may benefit from time alone to contemplate your own part in events. Switch off from the negativity.

Wednesday 23rd

You may wake up with a feeling that something must go today. This might be a deeply felt conviction that is no longer serving you. Stirrings from your deepest self may come to the surface to be dealt with. You feel adrift while this is happening.

Thursday 24th

Self-talk may confuse you as it veers more towards what you have failed to do and does not acknowledge your life achievements. Try to turn this around and look at how you have matured and grown through hard lessons. You are the most steadfast sign and your efforts are to be commended.

Friday 25th

Your inner compass is evading you now. The end goal is not in sight. This is because you need to concentrate on where you are now. Look around at the terrain and find your footing for this stage in the climb. You will soon feel supported again.

Saturday 26th

You have a boost of confidence and feel like yourself again. Goal-driven, sure-footed and aiming high. At times when you lose this, come back to centre and find reasons to be proud of yourself. Your journey never ends. The destination is not the end goal, your experience along the way is.

Sunday 27th

Today is a beautiful day for love. You have your dreams in sight and are meeting your own needs. There may be a mini-shift or you might let something go. This could be an old way of thinking that has held you back or a structure that gave no support.

Monday 28th

Your motto is 'onwards and upwards'. Nothing can hold you down for long. You may feel in complete alignment with your goals, your loves and your thinking today. Your head and heart are in sync. You might have some genius ideas about finances, so maybe you could talk to the boss.

MARCH
....

Tuesday 1st

Although you may begin the day with a feeling of being stuck, as the day progresses your communications lighten your mood. A few surprises could come your way through messages or short trips. These could bring you pleasure and allow some self-expression to sneak through your tough exterior.

Wednesday 2nd

A new moon highlights a new beginning in teaching, learning or your immediate environment. This can bring big positive change if you allow it. You may be conversing with spiritual people or going with the flow of a heartwarming group with a quest for something that expands your horizons.

Thursday 3rd

Be on the lookout for a very special person who can change your world view forever. You are in the spotlight now as the celestial lovers meet in your sign. You could be saying goodbye to a past love and focusing more on yourself, but you may also meet someone new.

Friday 4th

This is a day for contemplation, or if you feel like it, plotting your next moves. You have many ideas today and may wish to discuss these with family members, particularly parents. A sensitive, feminine perspective may help you to organise your thoughts and make a plan of action.

Saturday 5th

Today is blessed with very powerful planetary energy and
you should make the most of it. Golden opportunities are
presented to you now, which raise your status and self-esteem.
Love is highly likely and it is critical that you clear the path
if this is a new love interest.

Sunday 6th

Walk into today with a sense of gratitude, euphoria and a
willingness to be part of a bigger picture. Partnerships are
favoured if there is a shared vision. Love is in the air.
This may feel unreal and, deep down, you are frightened,
but step into the future with trust.

Monday 7th

If you feel the need to keep a guard up, do so, but be flexible.
The universe is conspiring to bring you out of yourself this
year and show you things you have only ever dreamed of.
Be open to a new way of experiencing pleasures without
compromising yourself.

Tuesday 8th

Look carefully and you may see a glimpse of the climb ahead.
From this perspective, it may look rosy and sunny, and you may
feel that this is an illusion. You are so used to hard work that you
have trouble accepting that a mountain can also be beautiful.

Wednesday 9th

With four planets hanging around in your area of self-worth,
you must sit up and listen. This is a time of change for you.
You may begin to review where you place value, what is
important to you and what drives you onwards. You must now
schedule a time for pleasure.

Thursday 10th

Are you feeling things shift? This might be your world view getting bigger and showing new heights to scale. You may need to take some time alone to process this and make small adjustments before taking huge leaps over to another mountain. Be sure you are free from idealist thinking.

Friday 11th

Today you are more sensitive than usual and aim to put your partner first. Conversations might be deep and meaningful. It's possible that you find an emotional side that you never knew you had. A special person or partner has found a soft spot of yours and you like it.

Saturday 12th

This is another great day if you're looking to impress someone. Love can bring pleasant surprises and may liberate you from old ways of relating. A mission or quest has new meaning now and you wish to involve people you care about.

Sunday 13th

The Sun is sitting on Neptune who acts as your inner compass. You may feel exactly in line with your true north. Illusions have been burned away and reality shows great things. You might still need to let something go with love or transform it in some way.

Monday 14th

You may have a day where your work-hard conscience kicks in and you doubt yourself. This can bring some shocks to the system, but as this is only a passing phase, you should feel all the feelings and acknowledge them. You must get used to no longer being a solo climber.

Tuesday 15th

If you are still having reservations, try to find your centre and hold yourself in that place today. Make no moves one way or the other. Be still, observe both sides and see what each does to your emotions, self-esteem and intentions. Stay neutral today if you can.

Wednesday 16th

Take some time today to look at your health. You may not have noticed if you've been neglecting yourself. If you have been living on high adrenaline recently, you may feel a little comedown and need time to reset. Get back into your routine and check long-term plans.

Thursday 17th

Pay attention today as this could be a roller-coaster ride of emotions. You may feel a little guilty that you are not putting enough effort into your career and that you have missed something. You might need to put your dreams on hold and go back and check some details.

Friday 18th

The full moon today has been bringing out your edginess.
However, look at your achievements now and celebrate them.
Your big plans may still be able to incorporate new ways of
thinking or being that you have developed. You will find a
way to do this.

Satruday19th

Enjoy the weekend with an individual or a group you care
about deeply. You may find that you need a little jolt to get out
of your low mood and negativity. Know that this self-talk will
tarnish the good things you are brewing up this year. Look on
the bright side.

Sunday 20th

The spring equinox arrives as the Sun dips into your family
area. This can be a great time for plans to be put into action
or made more secure. Try pausing and reflecting today before
planting those seeds. The equinox requires that you achieve
balance before tipping it.

Monday 21st

Whatever is going on in your head today may come out of your
mouth pretty quickly. Be very careful as there is a chance that
you spill a secret or share more than you need to. This may not
go down too well with people you are trying to impress.

Tuesday 22nd

Your social groups may be lively today and you may find some boundaries are breached. Stay safe online and avoid conflict if you can. You need to let something go and stop dwelling on it. Time alone is what you will need tonight. This will help you unwind and get back to your centre.

Wednesday 23rd

Listen very carefully for messages regarding your true north and direction in life. A recent passion, possibly one that you share with a special person or a group, is nagging at you. Do something about this. Act on it by joining your name or committing to group projects.

Thursday 24th

The little devil sitting on your shoulder is keeping you from being part of something worthwhile. Right now, you may want to be alone, but what about tomorrow? Sit with your feelings for now, but don't dismiss something that could bring you a lot of satisfaction in the long term.

Friday 25th

This is a time where you feel that you could have done something differently. You can't go back and do it again. What's done is done and you should take that as a lesson. Family may seek your attention today, but you need time to do something for yourself, too.

Saturday 26th

You may wake up with the knowledge that a change must be made. This may niggle at you all day, but you will work out what it is by evening. Speak to a few people in your close environment and get a clear picture of how your involvement in their shared vision will help.

Sunday 27th

You need to do some evaluating. Look at your home and your bank balance. They may both need a tidy up or a new look. Mercury will visit your family area, so you might try looking for advice from family elders. You may be irritable and restless.

Monday 28th

Another roller-coaster ride awaits you today. You think about what you want, what you desire and how you are going to get it. You may feel blocked or restricted. However, this can be resolved by tactic talks with someone you admire, and a balance achieved by the end of the day.

Tuesday 29th

You may be reaching out to others and enjoying unconditional love and comradeship today. It's possible that you are floating on a cloud of nostalgia. If there's no risk of harm, enjoy it. Spiritual groups may be of importance and take up your energy now.

Wednesday 30th

You may still be in a little bubble of bliss. Make sure that
you are safe and realistic as you tend to stray into hedonism.
Everything looks beautiful to you now but what happens when
you take off the rose-tinted spectacles? Stay grounded as that
is what you know best.

Thursday 31st

You have come back down to earth and set about planning,
co-ordinating and giving orders to some of your family
members. You may be switching up your home and making
changes that will benefit your tribe. Be practical or use your
head today. Be logical and rational.

APRIL
· · · · · · · · · · · · · · · · ·

Friday 1st

Listen to your heart today. A new moon will bring with it
more and more ideas and plans for you to initiate. You may
not be able to achieve all of them and some may be wild
dreams. What is your heart saying? Set about planning the
ones that move you the most.

Saturday 2nd

You may be eager to set wheels in motion today. This could
mean an adventure with a loved one or a solo luxury treat.
Look at all the rules and regulations before getting ahead of
yourself. Love, sex and pleasure are on the agenda for tonight.

Sunday 3rd

Your mind is so full of head noise today that you need to find
some peace somehow. It may be impossible to sort out your
self-talk from real conversations. You could be restless and
need to get things off your chest. Sometimes things are better
out than in.

Monday 4th

Be very careful today, as the energy suggests that you could
come up against a few brick walls. However much you believe
you are being inclusive, there may be someone feeling left out.
It could be you. Don't attempt to breach boundaries, but find
a workaround instead.

Tuesday 5th

Today is a day for love, not war. You may be pushing too hard to get what you want, when you should relax and let it willingly come your way. Sit tight and wait until this evening when the planet of love, Venus, moves into your communications area. Sweet talk is possible.

Wednesday 6th

You want to talk and get an idea of how you may be of service. This could be in your mundane daily life activities. Take a look at how you are working your routines. Do you need to fit in time for exercise or take care of your health?

Thursday 7th

It's possible that you are being a little too much for someone close. They may be tired of hearing your big dreams and would prefer to see you taking practical steps towards them. Partnerships may be more lenient tonight and allow you to dream in their arms.

Friday 8th

Try not to let your imagination run away with you today. Your dreams are even getting too big for you. You should check in with some grounded friends and get an opinion. Illusions may also be huge today, so watch out for anyone trying to trick you. Touch base with reality if you can.

Saturday 9th

You have a better perspective today. A sensitive person may have shown you that you are climbing a mountain with unknown terrain and need to keep checking the map. Slowly does it; you have a great team behind you and you must use them well.

Sunday 10th

Today could be tricky if you attempt to think too much. Your head and heart are not in sync and you may find that you have a tantrum about this. You might be seeking answers in all the wrong places and this is making you unfavourable amongst your peers. Rein it in now.

Monday 11th

Hold on to your hat as there is a chance that something big is going to happen. You may be offered a lift partway up your personal mountain. This could be beneficial or it could put you off track. Be prepared to scrutinise any help offered now.

Tuesday 12th

Take some time today to view your position. This is not a good time to take any action you may regret. It is imperative that you check every tiny detail twice. You might feel like you have missed a golden opportunity, but you may also have dodged a bullet.

Wednesday 13th

If you have lost your sense of harmony, take a step back. Something else will pop up today for you to deal with and this may radicalise the way you have been viewing a situation. Genius thinking combined with thorough checks will bring solutions to long-standing problems.

Thursday 14th

Try not to overthink a problem today. If it has not already been solved, let it go for now. You would do better by finishing up small jobs in the home or checking your bank balance. Bigger things can wait for another time. Sort out your immediate problems before the ambitious ones.

Friday 15th

There are now four planets in your communication area. This will be a good time to consider your partnerships and big world vision. Can you be a compassionate warrior and join good causes? You may even want to join a revolution of sorts. Spiritual groups will attract you more now.

Saturday 16th

Look at your career highlights over the last six months. How have you lifted yourself up to be noticed? A full moon today will show up where you have been recognised and appraised. Check that your home-work life is in balance. Lead the way.

Sunday 17th

Give your social groups some time today. You may be able to deepen a connection with one or more members. Intense, evocative subjects are piquing your interest and you have a desire to learn more. Sex, death and rebirth may light a spark in your psyche you have tried to ignore.

Monday 18th

The week begins with heavy energy. Filter your speech before it comes out of your mouth as it could shock others. You may be feeling outrageous and unconventional, and desire the shock factor. Hedonism is not the way to start the week.

Tuesday 19th

As the Moon shifts, you turn your attention to matters within you that you wish to explore. Exercise caution if you are doing text-book self-therapy as you may find yourself down a rabbit hole. Enjoy rooting around in the underworld, but don't touch anything or it may have the power to keep you there.

Wednesday 20th

You may be on a journey that has surreal twists and turns that you are not familiar with. You may be in danger of being enticed into something that isn't right for you. Keep grounded by doing practical things today and stay in touch with your physical body.

Thursday 21st

This morning, you feel more like yourself and can set about doing physical activity or enjoying cooking. You may wish to challenge yourself with a new recipe. Capricorns like to win and this will be good for you today. Climb a mini-mountain and reward yourself with the results.

Friday 22nd

There is delicious energy available for you to access if you wish. Love and dreams may be discussed with partners or written down as it comes from your mind and edited later. You need to go with the flow today. Dancing would be a lovely activity for you and a partner.

Saturday 23rd

You might have an emotional attachment to something that needs to be transformed. This could be your lifestyle or way of thinking. Perhaps it's time to change things up. You may have a desire to be a little more unconventional and move away from what is expected. Go with it.

Sunday 24th

Try not to take much notice of what anyone else thinks of you today. You may be more self-conscious if you have changed certain things. Watch what you say as there is a tendency to ask too many questions and then to question the answers. Your curiosity can be tiresome to others.

Monday 25th

You may hear your inner compass swaying in the wind today and as much as you'd like to grasp it, it evades you. Now is not the time to forge ahead. Balance what you have and who you have it with. Think of the collective and your part in it now.

Tuesday 26th

Tempers may flare today as your energy enables you to let off steam in some way. This would be better done at the gym than letting your words fly out at unsuspecting colleagues. On the other hand, you may find a project that fires up your passions.

Wednesday 27th

Enjoy this dreamy day and contact people close to you. This is a great time for one of the highest loves of all, the love for your fellow man. Sign up to a good cause and root for the underdog. Take back control of something that has been bothering you.

Thursday 28th

Listen to your self-talk today. You may hear about something that you can begin to do, such as a short course of study in your local area. Words of love can be expressed with ease, so perhaps you can start a poetry class. Be expressive and creative today, and enjoy it.

Friday 29th

Pluto turns retrograde in your sign. You may have become so used to this over the past years that you feel like you are constantly reinventing yourself. Make a special effort to reach out to someone special today, even if it's just by message or phone call. They need to know you're still there for them.

Saturday 30th

Make the most of the new moon and solar eclipse energy today. Be aware that this is a wild card and anything could happen. Romance and creativity are highlighted. If romance it is, then today is a great day to wine and dine someone special.

MAY

. . . .

Sunday 1st

You may wake up today with a restless energy or a feeling of
unfinished business. Is there something that needs to be said
concerning your love life? Don't leave it too late, or you could
find that you are giving false hopes and promises to someone
you care about. Be sensitive to other's needs now.

Monday 2nd

Duty calls today. It may be frustrating to speak from the heart
as you must make rational choices now. You have done the
groundwork in relationships and may find that a honeymoon
period is over and the harder work of sticking together begins.
Try to separate emotions from logic.

Tuesday 3rd

This may be a day filled with irritation for you. Your need to
connect with like-minded people may be thwarted by your
obligations and mundane duties. Try to put that energy into
what you're doing and be in the moment rather than thinking
ahead into the future hours.

Wednesday 4th

You are in a state of two minds and feel unsure of which way to
turn. You would much rather follow what your heart is saying
but you can't quite do it. Be careful that your frustration is not
aimed at someone who doesn't deserve it. Do some exercise
and get rid of excess energy.

Thursday 5th

Look to your one-to-one relationships to find a sense of calm. There is a powerhouse of energy building up in you and you need an outlet or some soothing. Today can result in genius thinking and a great new project may be initiated.

Friday 6th

Sweet-talking a lover or simply discussing future plans and obligations may be helpful today. You feel the need for a partner who can go along with your plans and bring some feeling into them. You too often think from a practical perspective that you forget to factor in how it might feel.

Saturday 7th

Relaxation comes easier now. You can dream and enjoy good fortune today as you feel perfectly in sync with the universe. Spiritual matters become very important to you. This may be because you've learnt to take time out for deep thinking and contemplation. Meditation could be good for you.

Sunday 8th

You might have found a way to work with that restless energy today. If you are mindful not to push or probe into a partner's mind too much, you may be able to deepen a commitment. You could also spend time doing something physical, such as a brisk walk outdoors together.

Monday 9th

After a nice weekend, you might be reluctant to settle into the working week. You may feel that authority figures are purposely trying to get in your way, but this is not the case. Your irritability returns and there is a chance that you have a tantrum. Be ready for this.

Tuesday 10th

Mercury turns retrograde today. You may have already felt this coming. Communications might be misunderstood and your mundane duties could give you a few hiccups. Double-check all travel plans and back up your technical devices. Take some time out if you are not feeling very sociable or agreeable.

Wednesday 11th

Work with what you have today and don't attempt anything new. If you start a new project now, it could be too big for you and will be abandoned, half done. The best thing you can do is concentrate on establishing loving bonds and making exciting plans with important people.

Thursday 12th

Be aware of your conversations at work today. You may feel an element of control or power struggles around you. You should be able to talk yourself out of a tricky situation, but will still have to deal with the fall-out. Aim to balance emotions and use tact in your professional arena.

Friday 13th

Look to your creative and romantic pursuits. The planetary energy is showing you what is worth your time and energy. This is a sneak peek into a possible future, should you choose to accept what you are seeing. How might you benefit long-term? Consider all options now.

Saturday 14th

Why not get dressed up and spend some time with your social groups today? This is a time when you feel the need for your closest friends. You may also seek your like-minded groups and engage in deeply intense conversations you are unable to have with your everyday colleagues.

Sunday 15th

Try not to neglect a love relationship today, as you may be getting too dependent on social groups. Spend some time figuring out where your passion and energy wants to go and make space for those who love you. If you rebel against this, it could cause some unwanted tension.

Monday 16th

Today, there is a full moon and lunar eclipse in your social area. You may well find that this super-intense energy brings up things that have been hidden from you. There could be gossip, nastiness or revelations about people who you once thought were on the same page as you.

Tuesday 17th

Let the aftermath of the eclipse settle for now and spend some time alone. You may need to process recent events before taking any action or making a judgement. Find the compassionate warrior within you and practise the pause before doing something you may regret. Introspection would be good for you today.

Wednesday 18th

You have an itch that needs scratching, but you need to learn to leave it alone. Your dreams and aspirations are fuelled by your passion to get them. You could be going all out to achieve something in the shortest time possible, but don't set yourself up to fail.

Thursday 19th

The Moon is in your sign and you may have to check in with yourself and get back your equilibrium. You are being observed and it is important that you use your restlessness and ambition wisely. Grounding is important now. Get to grips with the hard facts and continue climbing your personal mountain.

Friday 20th

You may have been able to temper your ambitious nature today, and are slowly and methodically making progress. Self-control is important. Mercury may cause you some big problems in your daily routines, but if you stay mindful, you can overcome them.

Saturday 21st

Today, it is important to stay alert and listen for messages or instructions. These may come from your higher mind or from dreams, but are nevertheless important. You could experience some brain-fog, which makes clarity hard to come by, but just let it pass until you are sure of how to proceed.

Sunday 22nd

Money may be a theme for today. This could come in the form of a windfall or it could be that you are investing in a good cause. Watch that it doesn't distract from your daily duties or there will be some catching up to do.

Monday 23rd

Mercury retreats into your creative and romantic area of life. You now need to review things you have been busy or passionate about. Be respectful if this causes problems in your love life. It may be a chance to cover ground you should have done earlier this year.

Tuesday 24th

Tricky energy may cause you to act without thinking today. There might be some harsh words spoken and a tendency to switch off and avoid conflict. You may be too emotional, so step back until this energy passes.

Wednesday 25th

Your natural family values are amped up now and you know that you need to pay more attention to this area of life. You may see elders in the family laying down the law or bringing in something that benefits all. You see the sense in this and go along with it.

Thursday 26th

Rules and regulations are working well for you. You appreciate the structure they bring and don't feel the need to rebel, at least not yet. This may be new territory, but you are willing to give it a go. You may even find that this helps to solve long-standing problems.

Friday 27th

You may have a short and sharp crisis of conscience today. Changes have been made and for these to happen, something has had to go. It is okay to mourn this loss and let it go lovingly. Remember that space has been made for new growth and progression.

Saturday 28th

The planet of love, Venus, moves into her home, which is your creative and romantic area. You will feel this today as you rediscover something you are passionate about and pay it some attention. This could be an art project or a love relationship. Beautiful things are coming your way.

Sunday 29th

You get in touch with your inner compass today and see that your future looks bright. The climb up your personal mountain will be interesting. You are so emotionally invested in this that you risk saying something to the wrong person at the wrong time. Stay silent today.

Monday 30th

Today, there is a new moon and solar eclipse. This closes the window of the past month, but opens up new opportunities for you to learn, teach or research something you are passionate about. You may be more driven than usual to get started on projects or speak to new people.

Tuesday 31st

Stick to the rules. You might have a newfound appreciation for authority figures, who can guide you into a new way of thinking without going over the top. Put aside your dreams and listen to others with more experience. You could learn something important.

JUNE
· · · · · · · · · · · · · · · ·

Wednesday 1st
Concentrate on what you need from one-to-one relationships.
What do you lack, that another brings to your life? You may
find some resistance or discord within your family life and
veer towards the sensitivity a special person can bring you.
Allow this to relax you.

Thursday 2nd
You may have a pleasant surprise or two today. Inspiration can
come to you from unusual places and help you to progress
with your creative or romantic pursuits. You might have an
'Aha!' moment, which turns your attention to something that
has been bothering you.

Friday 3rd
Mercury turns direct now and will help you verbalise or
process something you have discovered recently. You may find
a muse and put pen to paper. A desire to know more about
a tricky topic can be satisfied if you are respectful of other
people's boundaries.

Saturday 4th
It's possible that you feel like a blockage has been removed
and you get the go-ahead on family matters. There is enough
energy and joy within your family unit to make this a happy
day. However, your ruler, Saturn, turns retrograde and will
teach you something new about finances and value.

Sunday 5th

You may have touched upon a sore point with a partner and have reached a stalemate situation. This will pass, so hold tight. You don't have to know everything at once. Leave room for improvement and give each other some space before continuing this line of enquiry. Be gentle and compassionate.

Monday 6th

You can't have it all your own way. If you feel that there are things you need to get off your chest, consider that someone else does too. You may need to look at your own expectations before making a judgement on a loved one. Money matters may also be a problem.

Tuesday 7th

Today, there is better energy to call a truce, make an apology and get loved up with your partner. Put all cards on the table and ensure that everyone knows all the facts. Egos may be a little hurt, but it is time to put someone else first.

Wednesday 8th

Take things easy today as you may find that your energy is drained easily. Check in with your health and make sure that you are getting enough rest and exercise. You may feel more balanced by this evening if you take stock. Fill your own cup before sharing with others.

Thursday 9th

You may still be feeling low on energy. This can be a depressing day if your spirits remain clouded and moody. Forget what needs to be done; use the day to take care of immediate needs. Family members may require your attention, but they will have to wait.

Friday 10th

Friends and shared interest groups can lift you up today. Use them well. You may have already learned something from Saturn regarding what is important and what can wait. Plan some fun time or a social activity and let negativity drain away. Be open to something new that may be offered.

Saturday 11th

Social groups continue to build up your strength and light a few fires of passion. Your romantic pursuits are favoured now and you may have a few delicious surprises. Do what feeds your soul today, as this is a rare chance for you to step down from work life.

Sunday 12th

There is no need to feel guilty about having fun. You may be conflicted today and regret spending time in one place this weekend. Try to connect with your inner compass and realign yourself with your long-term goals. Then, make short-term steps to get there.

Monday 13th

Retreat from outside activity for a short time. Recharging your batteries is in your best interest now. This is a time for introspection but also to reconnect with spirit and your belief system. Make short and sweet messages to your tribe and tell them you will be back when you are refreshed.

Tuesday 14th

A full moon has the effect of showing you what your deepest psyche needs to heal. You may wish to climb higher mountains or foreign ones, but those closer to home need to be conquered first. Your dreams have not been abandoned; they are being adjusted and made more attainable.

Wednesday 15th

You may be frustrated today as you don't seem to have any joy or optimism left. This is because you are probably still depleted and haven't given yourself enough rest. Find something that you enjoy, such as a favourite book or TV show, and let yourself binge on it.

Thursday 16th

A little loving may come your way even if you initiate it. Soften your edges and allow this in. You need it. If you can't seem to find your true north, let it go and come back another day. Treat yourself to good food and nourishment.

Friday 17th

At last, your hope and joy are back. You may now see the benefits of rest and recuperation. Mountains will always be there, but your health won't. You may have also got a financial boost, which will cheer you up. Look outwards and give gratitude to your support groups now.

Saturday 18th

Today, you are willing to forgo a weekend of pleasure and listen to the harder lessons of life. You may evaluate what Saturn has taught you so far. Think about the things you value most and how you treat them. Do you take them for granted or are you truly thankful for them?

Sunday 19th

You may have an urge to find a spiritual outlet today. This might be for you to give thanks where it is due or to merge with spiritual people who have a faith you crave. This may be difficult for you to discuss with those closest to you.

Monday 20th

Your inner compass is right in front of you today. Check in with it and ensure that you are on track. Little mundane jobs can be finished in good time for you to indulge in some 'me' time and make lists and plans for the future. Write down your dreams and visions.

Tuesday 21st

The summer solstice marks a time where you are more connected to your loved one. The longest day gives you enough light to look clearly at where you may need to make necessary changes for the better. Talk and think big today, if just to lift your spirits.

Wednesday 22nd

There is only one way to feel today. Driven. You have set your sights on the next summit and you are raring to go. Make sure that you are well prepared for this. Look at your family group for support, check out the terrain and go for it. Take one step at a time, though!

Thursday 23rd

You may be moving much slower than you would like. There is no need to rush as this personal mountain has much to teach you. Something is not right for you at the moment and is weighing you down, so let it go lovingly and lighten your load.

Friday 24th

This is a day where you may have ideas spilling out of you. Love and sensual activity can be electrifying. Be warned though, this energy may also make you super-restless and argumentative. Try to channel it positively or you will regret any outbursts at a later date.

Saturday 25th

Stop, look and listen to what is around you. You may have missed a golden opportunity or forged on ahead without some essential information. Connect to your true north and observe the landscape. Do you need to go back for something? Have you packed enough nourishment?

Sunday 26th

If you get all your mundane duties done early today, you might spend the remainder of the weekend in a state of bliss with someone special. They may have a short lesson about how you serve others and they serve you. Look at your obligations now. Have you neglected any?

Monday 27th

Today would be a good time to do a little research about what you are tied to. You may be able to tweak your responsibilities in a way that suits everyone involved and frees up some time for you. Don't fall into a scapegoat relationship with someone now; let them share the responsibilities.

Tuesday 28th

Neptune, the planet who is your inner compass, turns retrograde now and will hide away for a while. You will have to work much harder to connect now. This will enable you to slow down and focus on the journey more than the destination. Look for who helps and who hinders.

Wednesday 29th

A very sensitive full moon falls in your relationship area.
Things might come to light that cause hurt, or you could find
that you've reached a plateau with someone. Tears may present
themselves if egos are wounded. Take care of each other.

Thursday 30th

You may experience control issues or power struggles now.
This is a rest stop along your way and a lesson to learn.
Neptune is eluding you as you try to grasp your inner compass
and get aligned. There is too much fog at the moment, so stop,
rest and process the journey so far.

JULY

· · · · · · · · · · · · · · · · · · ·

Friday 1st

If you want to have your say over the weekend, there is a good chance you may be heard and acknowledged. However, there is a risk that you overinflate your ego and can be too much for some. Take into account all that you need to do before introducing something else.

Saturday 2nd

You may find that you are backtracking today and reconsidering things you have said. The planetary energy turns very challenging now. Back off until you have more clarity and acceptance from others involved. You may have pushed through a boundary and upset someone. An apology could be required.

Sunday 3rd

There is a push and pull feel today and you may need to flow with it for a while. This will be beneficial if you are in the mood to negotiate and compromise. Try to think of another perspective. Be methodical and analytical now.

Monday 4th

If you are feeling as if you have missed a chance or neglected something, put that right today. Your energy is great for finishing up projects or talks within your family and home. You may have a last-minute push to do some home improvements or visit people you have missed.

Tuesday 5th

The energy shifts today and you may feel more settled. Communication will be improved between lovers and your personal drive heads towards romantic and creative projects. You now have more determination to change things around and give yourself some pleasure. This may be around the home or with a love partner.

Wednesday 6th

What is it that doesn't feel right? You might have a niggling feeling that something is out of balance. This could be your home and work lives, but as this is just a passing phase, don't make any big changes. Take note and think about it for now.

Thursday 7th

Today, you manage to work around restrictions or blockages and get all your duties done with time to spare. An evening alone won't go amiss as you may use that time to treat yourself and check in with your body and health. Are you taking care of your own needs?

Friday 8th

You might feel that your identity is being threatened or you have some moments of self-doubt. This may have been a familiar theme to you over the last few years, but you have always come out of it successfully. Let the mood pass and don't think too much about it.

Saturday 9th

Friends and lovers may cause you to feel conflicted. How would you prefer to spend your time this weekend? Whichever way you choose will upset the other. Intense times and friction make you irritable and you find that you reminisce about so-called easier times. Let that stay in the past.

Sunday 10th

You're desperately trying to connect with your inner compass as a way of avoiding having to deal with conflict or change. The best thing you can do today is to spend time alone and process your thoughts. Give yourself a break from outside distractions and get in touch with your inner world.

Monday 11th

You may not feel in the mood to climb a hill today, let alone a mountain. There is much you wish to know and maybe you have let a line of enquiry or study slip. Maybe you don't have all the facts. An elder or teacher can help.

Tuesday 12th

The Moon slips into your sign and you feel a little more settled today. Your energy picks up as you have the attention of someone you like a great deal. This person can lift your mood and you forget about your recent woes. Enjoy the company of someone special.

Wednesday 13th

A full moon in your sign may come as a welcome relief. This can mark the completion of a six-month climb and show you off in a good light. You may get recognition for a job well done and you should reap the rewards. However, don't be tempted to show off.

Thursday 14th

You may wake with an uneasy feeling today. The energy is not easy, but you can work it to your advantage. This might be the best time to take on the words of an elder or a professional and let them guide you. Look to your wider groups for support.

Friday 15th

You may be struggling with a long-standing problem and getting nowhere with it. This may also be a repeated pattern that you just can't shift. Sit tight and think about your own responses and behaviour to certain situations. Are you open-minded enough to shift your perspective?

Saturday 16th

If you feel as if there is a lack of communication with a lover or professional partner, learn to sit and listen. It is time for you to be a little more sensitive and take on a nurturing role. Today can be quite emotional and you may be the shoulder someone needs to lean on.

Sunday 17th

What are your dreams telling you? You may have some ideas and plans that you would like to communicate with a loved one. Talking may bring a breakthrough and a new level may be reached. Be open and honest. Respect needs to be earned.

Monday 18th

Venus enters your relationship sector; watch how you have more compassion and desire for one another now. Shared dreams are likely to excite you both and you may make small changes to enhance your relationship. As always, be mindful of a partner's opinions and don't dismiss what they say.

Tuesday 19th

Whatever your mood today, it is sure to be large. You may be filled with ideas for activating dreams and shared visions, but don't get ahead of yourself as you will run out of steam. As a Capricorn, you know that the best-laid plans are made one step at a time.

Wednesday 20th

If you don't slow down, you will see that egos are clashing, and you are getting nowhere fast. It's best that you focus on your personal plans today and not those that involve another. Get your own jobs done and put down the roots of other plans if necessary.

Thursday 21st

You are in the mood for love and may take any slight rejection too personally. Remember that not everyone has the same energy at the same time. If you desire to spend time with a loved one, let them know and let them come to you.

Friday 22nd

It's likely that you are bursting at the seams today. All of your pistons are firing up and you want to start the race now. Whatever is holding you back must be respected as it is teaching you a valuable lesson. Wait for your green light or you may be penalised.

Saturday 23rd

Get all your mundane duties done early today as there is time and opportunity to play for most of the day. Your enthusiasm has calmed slightly but is no less potent. With a bit of luck, you can get a partner on board for a fun weekend. Ensure that you are both on the same page.

Sunday 24th

This may be your lucky weekend. You may be wining, dining and talking through the night. A bubble surrounds you, and the outside world and working week are a million miles away. This is great as you are being present and not aiming ahead as you usually do.

Monday 25th

You come back down to earth with a horrible bump today. The working week begins and knocks you from your happy place. However, your partner still needs your attention and the Moon is in the right place for you. Time to let them do the nurturing and protecting.

Tuesday 26th

Things may get just a little too comfortable today and end up having the reverse effect. Someone is being smothered and another is being needy. If you like this kind of thing then you feel loved and nurtured. However, it may make you cringe and run for the hills.

Wednesday 27th

All is forgiven today and the planetary energy makes it easier for you to relate healthily. You may have a glimpse of your true north and remember what it is that makes you tick. Restless energy can be channelled in a positive way today. Use it well.

Thursday 28th

A new moon gives you a chance to make plans and goals regarding intimate connections and how you might shine within them. Set intentions to have more laughs and playtime. Jupiter turns retrograde and you may need to turn some of your attention to your family for a few months.

Friday 29th

There is every possibility that you get involved in fights, conflicts and disagreements today. You may be expressing yourself in a manner that others will neither agree with nor condone. Prepare to be knocked back today, but you will give as good as you get. Watch that temper.

Saturday 30th

Your mouth may run away with you now, so try to pause and think before you respond. You will find that blocks are there for a reason, but you may have a toddler tantrum nonetheless. Use this energy to analyse your thoughts and habits instead. Take time to process things.

Sunday 31st

It may take a while, but there is an innovative idea trying to get out of your head and down on paper today. This may be a solution that can help you move forward in a grand way. Look at your romantic and creative pursuits for clues.

AUGUST

Monday 1st

Getting together with a lover can be explosive today. Sexual energy and romance are very high on the agenda. You may believe that this person is your whole future, but don't be distracted by what may turn out to be an illusion and rose-tinted glasses. Keep it real.

Tuesday 2nd

You are still pushing love relationships to their edge. This can be a good thing, but you must ensure that your partner wants this, too. Remember that you are both independent of each other and that the relationship you share is a separate entity. Enjoy the dynamics without becoming pushy or demanding.

Wednesday 3rd

Love and romance are still sizzling with intensity. The celestial lovers, Venus and Mars, are still making a helpful connection to your chart. However, you must not neglect your other duties and be sidetracked, as this will not look good in the workplace. Be a responsible lover and career person.

Thursday 4th

The intensity amps up, but your attention could now be drawn to your wider interest groups and friendships. You may be doing some research regarding topics you have not previously considered. Change is in the air and your old way of thinking may be challenged now. Prepare to broaden your mind.

Friday 5th

You may feel a little sluggish as your emotional mind takes you back to times past. Old wounds may surface, and you must think of these as triggers that will help you heal and grow. These may play on your mind this evening and cause you unrest.

Saturday 6th

Thinking about your past reopens wounds today. This may spoil your current good status in your romantic relationship. There may be a tendency to dream or a need to be alone and lick your wounds. Love is waiting for you if you can shrug off this low mood.

Sunday 7th

You may find yourself thinking and analysing too much today. Self-love is necessary for you to forgive ghosts from the past and move on. Take time to evaluate what is important to you and use that as a starting point. Be true to yourself and always act for the highest good.

Monday 8th

You may feel that you are being whisked away from your true north and begin to resent others. This is a passing phase and you may not be emotionally detached enough to think clearly. There is a fog around your inner compass. Wait for it to disperse before making judgements.

Tuesday 9th

You may attach blame to another person as an avoidance tactic. This can make you feel manipulated and resentful. Try to think with your logical and rational self, as you are better that way. Your sense and perception are off when you think from the heart. Talk with someone you trust.

Wednesday 10th

It is imperative that you regain your self-control. Your recent troublesome thoughts may cause a make-or-break situation in your love life. The sexual energy you wish to express may be mistaken for a lack of love and respect for another person. Make your mind up today.

Thursday 11th

You can't fight fire with fire. You may be unstable and volatile today. Mood swings are likely and people will avoid you if they can. This is a challenging day for you, so the best you can do is to spend time alone doing what feeds your soul.

Friday 12th

A full moon throws a spotlight over your current mindset. You desire to be open-minded and you yearn for freedom. You may have been struggling with attachment issues and letting your feelings for a special person guide you. In this process, you believe that you have lost your sense of self.

Saturday 13th

Your heart and head are not in sync today. Don't run the risk of saying something you will regret later. Accept that your thinking may be muddled or clouded. Ground yourself and do something you enjoy to take your mind to other things. Distraction with paperwork may be the answer.

Sunday 14th

You may manage to step up and out of your low mood today. If you can see a glimpse of your true north and get back into alignment, you will feel better about yourself. Your energy, drive and passion return, and you may be ready to accept a new challenge.

Monday 15th

Communication is the key today. You may have sorted out
what you want and what you need, and how a love relationship
might fit into this. New levels could be reached with a
lover, which can deepen your connection and bring a better
understanding of each other.

Tuesday 16th

Family issues seem to have grounded you and given you a solid
base. Feeling support from your immediate environment gives
you the strength to climb your mini mountains of success.
Remember to check each step on the way up and enjoy the
adventure. Words of love can delight you today.

Wednesday 17th

How would you like to be wooed? You may be thinking about
your own personal needs and what gives you pleasure. Talking
about this with a lover may feel selfish, but it is a necessary
part of relating and getting to know someone. You have needs
too and are entitled to express them.

Thursday 18th

There may be a sense of urgency today as you wish to ensure
that everything is okay with a lover or special person. Talking
about holidays or travel will be a useful and harmless way of
placing your relationship in the future months with something
to look forward to.

Friday 19th

Let yourself drift a little, but keep one foot on the ground. You may
notice that a mindful approach to the day allows you to relax and
not be so hard on yourself. Prepare for the coming weekend with a
resolve to be cheerful and cooperative. Stay open and flexible.

Saturday 20th

You may surprise yourself today as you want to talk all day long. Many topics are going around in your head and you can't decide which to discuss. Make sure that your mundane duties are done first. There will be plenty of time for debates and brainstorming later.

Sunday 21st

Logic and reason may fail you today. You may have exhausted your lines of enquiry or have returned to the starting point. Don't struggle with this; it's not that important. Sometimes, a circular discussion brings its own realisations. Spend the remainder of the weekend in your body and heart.

Monday 22nd

There is still that nagging feeling that you have something to get off your chest. It may be a confession, a deep desire or a complaint. Be sure not to direct this at someone you don't want to upset. Find an elder you respect to help you with this one.

Tuesday 23rd

The Sun heats up your desire to travel or learn something new. You may be thinking about higher education and doing all your research now. There might be a last-minute chance to get out and explore another country, or to broaden your mind with religion and philosophy.

Wednesday 24th

Uranus turns retrograde today and will affect your romantic and creative pursuits. You may find that you backtrack or feel restricted. This may be a rebellious phase where you wish to break free and do your own thing, or try something new and radical in love and art.

Thursday 25th

There is something you need to complete today. This might concern being analytical, thought processes or checking your research on travel and education. You may have a deadline you have forgotten about. Make this a priority today so you don't miss your chance. Keep emotions out and use your head.

Friday 26th

You might wake up today with exciting plans for the weekend. This may involve a partner or someone you share interests with. You have a restless energy and may rebel against any restrictions today. Use this energy wisely and problem-solve, or try a new way of doing something.

Saturday 27th

A new moon is a good omen for you today. It is a chance to temper your restlessness with a schedule, or plan to try something new. You may feel at odds and unsure about this, but trust that your bubbly energy is about to burst into a worthwhile new passion.

Sunday 28th

You might have to choose between self-love and love for all around you today. You are being tested about what you place value on. This may also include spending money and making a choice to spend it on an investment or something frivolous. Don't barter short-term gains for long-term ones.

Monday 29th

If you think that you have been sidetracked and have over-committed yourself, think again. You may be putting your own needs and desires first, but also balancing them with the world outside your door. Your head and heart are in sync, and know what is best for you today.

Tuesday 30th

Today, there is a push-and-pull energy, which can be tricky for you. Family demand your attention, but your heart is elsewhere. Be mindful of your responsibilities and obligations, but take time for yourself too. Give others a respectful 'No' if you are being asked to give more than necessary.

Wednesday 31st

You may be pulled into power struggles that do not really involve you. Stay away from the drama and let people know you will not be dragged into toxicity. The evening can become intense and your friendship groups may be the pot where this trouble is brewing.

SEPTEMBER
. . . .

Thursday 1st

Intense times may see the need for letting something go or
releasing someone from your past. It's no good hanging onto
what no longer serves your best interests. This may feel as if
it has been done in spite, but will ultimately bring you more
space for the new.

Friday 2nd

You may be troubled by disturbances in your romantic or
friendship connections. If you need to say something that
may cause conflict, do it in the kindest way possible. This is
not easy for you, but if you stay mindful and respectful, then
it shouldn't be too difficult.

Saturday 3rd

Spending some quiet time alone would be best for you this
weekend. You may not be very sociable and might need to be
introspective and process your thoughts and feelings. This may
be an ideal time to make schedules concerning how you would
like to use your energy.

Sunday 4th

Make sure that you have not overlooked anything regarding
shared finances or intimacy. Your dealings with a partner
may need some necessary adjustments before moving onto a
different level of commitment. Aim for balance and harmony,
but speak your mind with compassion. Don't let yourself be
taken for granted today.

Monday 5th

The Moon arrives back in your sign and you feel that all eyes are on you. Your social status is important to you, so always remain responsible and respectful. Be careful what you say. If it isn't kind, true or helpful, stay silent. You could be of service to others today.

Tuesday 6th

There is helpful energy available for you to act in a professional manner and make necessary changes. Transformations or changes of opinion will be looked on favourably. If there is any chance that tension arises, use it creatively to solve problems and get a sense of fairness.

Wednesday 7th

Money matters may need your attention today. You have the right frame of mind to organise your valuables or finances in a better way. You may notice that your mood has softened and you are looking out to the wider world to see how you may be of assistance in group ventures.

Thursday 8th

If you come up against a brick wall, stay there and contemplate why. This is a chance for you to use your inventive qualities and work a way around it. It will prove challenging and will require hard work, but there is nothing a Capricorn likes more than a new mountain to climb.

Friday 9th

You are likely feeling more of a connection to mankind today. You may have found a place where you can bring your skillset and put it to good use for the wider community. Messages and conversations intrigue you.

Saturday 10th

A full moon highlights how you have made your world bigger this year. Mercury turns retrograde and may give you some trouble in the workplace. This is a chance to redo, review and reset the balance between your work and home lives. Your inner compass is showing you what needs to be done.

Sunday 11th

You may not be able to think clearly today so ask for advice. There may be an elder in the family who can give you the clarity you seek. Look at things from a different perspective. A knowledgeable teacher or guru is what you need right now.

Monday 12th

This is a day where you are driven and get things done. You power through the day and tick many things off your checklist. Others will notice your professionalism and sense of responsibility. This is a productive start to the week. Be proud of yourself and claim a reward.

Tuesday 13th

You may be on a roll and getting things done. Make time for relaxation and love this evening. If you are alone, then treat yourself to a tasty meal, your favourite TV show or a beauty treatment. Sit back and allow yourself a moment of pride in what you have achieved.

Wednesday 14th

The restless energy surfaces again to make you look for more work to do. You may have an idea of what the future looks like for you and a partner, and take steps towards it. Time spent with a lover can be earth-shaking.

Thursday 15th

Today, you get a glimpse of your true north as the Sun burns away the mists. You feel very much in line with your path and are pleased with yourself. Simply enjoy this moment and don't worry about the summit. At this point, the journey is more important.

Friday 16th

Watch out for disagreements between men and women today. There may be a difference of opinion that can't be resolved just yet. Think of this as a holding space to put all your cards on the table for review. Don't be tempted to make a judgement call yet; just review all possible options.

Saturday 17th

The tension ramps up as you now feel emotionally attached to your opinions and outcomes. Suddenly, everything looks glum and hopeless. Trust that this is just a rest stop on the mountain and it may just be a rainy day. Check in with your body and health as you may be draining your resources.

Sunday 18th

Love relationships may suffer today as the energy suggests that communication and fairness are overlooked. Remember that Mercury is retrograde and you are asked to go over old ground before moving on. Double-check any travel plans and allow extra time for making short trips.

Monday 19th

Today, you might have managed to make progress and feel a little happier. This may be because you have looked at all the details and can be logical and rational. Emotionally, you simply need to be fair and just. Keep feelings out of decision-making.

Tuesday 20th

You may be a stubborn old goat today because you are forced to change your standpoint on something. If you can do this, you will soon see that there is a better way than the one you were clinging to. Bring something to a close now.

Wednesday 21st

Deep feelings may be triggered today. Your job is to recognise what the triggers are and what sore spots they are touching. You may want to shout and scream about how you have been hurt. The energy suggests that they may be healed if you can look at them objectively.

Thursday 22nd

You have the right kind of energy to start a fitness regime or to work on a health issue. It may be that you have been depleted recently and this has made you unhappy. Get on your feet and find your balance again. You may even begin to dance.

Friday 23rd

Mercury in retrograde is in the heart of the Sun today. Your job is to listen out for any messages, which may come from unlikely sources or from the dream world. You need to go even further back into an issue regarding travel or education and review it before moving on.

Saturday 24th

Today may feel a bit like you are stranded without a map. Sit still and enjoy the view. There will be time to get up and move when you have surveyed the territory and made mental notes. This is just as important as physical progress, so don't berate yourself for it.

Sunday 25th

A new moon is the reason you needed to stop and slow down.
It was not the time to move, but now it is. You may have a day
where conversations with a loved one are misunderstood, but
are quickly cleared up again. A balancing, harmonising moon
wants you to have mutual respect.

Monday 26th

Venus and Mercury meet up, giving you the perfect chance
to talk into the small hours with a partner. Remember that
Mercury is still retrograde, and you will need to speak with
precision and clarity. This goes for listening, too. Take time to
hear what the other is saying.

Tuesday 27th

This is an important day for hidden messages to be revealed.
It may be that someone's agenda is not in line with yours.
You will need to reassess this if it has been a big part of shared
plans. Make adjustments or transformations if you can.

Wednesday 28th

Look to your wider interest groups today. You may find the
inspiration you have been looking for. It may be the ideal place
to follow interests that could be outside the norm. Getting
your mind into something surreal or taboo will take you away
from minor problems if just for a short while.

Thursday 29th

Unrest or conflict may cause you to release something from
the past. It may also bring it back up into your consciousness.
This may be uncomfortable, but remember, it was in the past
once and it can be again. Ask yourself why it is resurfacing
now? What has triggered it?

Friday 30th

Let your energy drop and then relax into some introspection.
This may help you to process a few things. If you need to sleep
more than usual, do it. You need to find inner harmony within
for the next round of the journey. Be good to yourself now,
with nurturing and nourishment.

OCTOBER

Saturday 1st

You may be feeling under the weather and in no mood to socialise. Your energy is turned inwards and that's where it will stay today. You may be irritable with others and unable to get a grip on your personal mountain. Lie low and recuperate. Take some time off.

Sunday 2nd

Mercury turns direct today and you may get a flash of realisation. Your true north sits directly opposite and awakens you with a jolt. Suddenly, you know exactly where you wish to go and how to do it. You may be rather bold and slightly aggressive about getting your own way.

Monday 3rd

Today, you may find that you are drawing on skills learned in the past to help you move forward now. The trick is not to depend on them as there are newer skills to acquire. What you have mastered before is useful, but the world is waiting for you to evolve.

Tuesday 4th

This is a day where you may feel as if you have grown a new skin. You may be out there and witnessed by others as an oddity. You have a confidence that is envied by some, as you are ready to take bold steps and climb high.

Wednesday 5th

Your motor is running, and you may check the map before setting off. It will be useful to schedule time with a boss or authority figure and get them on your team. Someone is ready to support you in your endeavours if you agree to play by the rules.

Thursday 6th

Today is a day for networking and connecting with allies. You may wish to merge spiritually with like-minded folk who share your bigger vision. Try to stay grounded as under this energy, you may wander off into fantasy thinking and make insurmountable goals for yourself.

Friday 7th

Messages and information are important to convey today. You will find that some information may be discarded and some can be filed away. Listen to your inner voice for direction and trust that your higher self is guiding you. This is a good time to meditate or connect with your spiritual path.

Saturday 8th

There may be setbacks and doubts entering your mind. This will be challenging after you have been so keen to get going. Know that this phase will pass soon and if you have already done some groundwork, it will still be sufficient for the journey. Speak to experienced elders now.

Sunday 9th

You have the green light today. A full moon shines in your family area, and you are admired and applauded for your persistence. Pluto also turns direct, meaning that you are now free to make huge changes and transform the old into something new. Follow your heart today.

Monday 10th

Have you been interested in a course of higher education recently? You could make enquiries and see if this still suits you. You may find that you grieve over something you have had to leave behind. This is natural. Allow yourself to deal with what emotions this brings up.

Tuesday 11th

Your career goals may receive a boost today. It may be that your high aspirations have been witnessed by influential people and you are being recommended for a new role. The future is bright, and you are becoming more and more emotionally invested in it. Keep your eyes forward and stay focused.

Wednesday 12th

You may experience more roadblocks that cause your temper to flare. You wonder why you are not getting a break. This isn't true and you are simply being hard on yourself. You must look at these hold-ups as a chance to rest and review the territory. You might also take time for fun.

Thursday 13th

Concentrate on your duties and obligations today. You must not neglect what you need to do and, likewise, you should not neglect your health. Check in with your body and give yourself an M.O.T. Schedule appointments that you may have missed recently.

Friday 14th

You could have an emotional pull towards sorting out your finances and possessions today. This may simply be a decluttering exercise, during which you find it hard to get rid of stuff. Your home will be a fresh space when you have finished, and it will bring you great joy and pride.

Saturday 15th

Today, your energy levels are directed at your lover or important relationships. This is an area you may have neglected recently, and you need to reconnect lovingly. You may be more open to one-on-one relationships than large social activity. Let yourself be nurtured and protected by another.

Sunday 16th

You are not in the right mindset to use logic and reason today. No matter; enjoy the day and just do what feeds your soul. This may be intense conversations, loving sex or good food. However, be careful not to overdo the good stuff or push the boundaries of someone you care about.

Monday 17th

Reluctantly, you begin the working week. You may still be on cloud nine and refusing to come down. This is just a typical case of Monday morning blues and you will get over it by evening. Only do what is necessary. Anything extra can wait until tomorrow.

Tuesday 18th

Today can act as a reset in your relationships. You may find that when relating on a deeper level, there isn't much progress. However, today you may go back to a comfortable level and begin to build anew. Take it slowly; don't frighten a partner by exposing your darkest secrets too soon.

Wednesday 19th

There is a high chance that you shock or upset someone today. Be very careful how you tread and use those Capricorn skills of balancing on a ledge without moving. If you must retreat or back down, then do so. You may need to be humble today.

Thursday 20th

The energy today is so sweet that you will think you are in a chocolate box. It may feel surreal to you, but learn to enjoy it as this doesn't come around too often. You may be a people pleaser today or you may just be on a delicious new level with a lover.

Friday 21st

The lovely feeling continues long enough for you to enjoy whistling while you work. Others may become infected by your happy mood and this spreads around you. This is a pleasant day, in which you are methodical and happy to be of service to those you care about.

Saturday 22nd

Your energy lifts and you give people a few surprises. Your love life will benefit, as will your demeanour. You have lost sight of your inner compass, but that's fine. You are learning to enjoy the view at this current moment in time. Have a great day.

Sunday 23rd

Your ruler, Saturn, turns direct today. This is the end of the tough lessons for you this year. What did you learn about responsibilities with money and belongings? The energy now shifts to an intense time with social groups. Expect many invitations to private soirees or groups.

Monday 24th

This is a great day for networking and research. Career advancement will benefit if you are able to sign yourself up for new courses or different duties. Show then what you are made of and keep climbing the corporate ladder. This is what you are good at.

Tuesday 25th

There is a very intense new moon and solar eclipse today. This will open a window into your wider social groups and you may find great new ideas pouring through. Females are highlighted, so listen to what the wise women in your groups are saying. You may feel more empathic and nurturing now.

Wednesday 26th

Something is stirring between your creative and romantic activities. You may be brewing up a fascinating new project that is ready to be born. This may go against the grain of your duties or shake things up at home. Be respectful and mindful of what changes this may bring.

Thursday 27th

You may be fired up and ready to do something bold. However, you need more time to process your thoughts before shouting them out. Get advice and take some time alone today. Keep quiet for now. It may be useful to build a vision board and see things depicted this way.

Friday 28th

What have you forgotten? You are ready for a big quest, but may have a niggling feeling that you have overlooked something. This could give you an emotional tug as it may be a neglected person or a conversation that you should have had a long time ago. Act on it now.

Saturday 29th

The intensity amps up as you are bursting to talk to others about new plans, projects or love affairs. Hold on a little longer, if you can. You may even find that a confidante has beaten you to it and already spilt the beans. Watch out for jealousy in your groups.

Sunday 30th

Mars turns retrograde today. You will be reminded that you are not invincible and, as a Capricorn, you need to take things slowly. This may be frustrating for you, but you are at risk of becoming ill if you rush. This is a chance to put your health first and foremost.

Monday 31st

It is important that you get a measure of self-control today. You may be grasping for your inner compass and feeling a little adrift. It could be helpful to connect with your spiritual friends or those who have experienced similar things to you. Money is an issue today, too.

NOVEMBER
· · · · · · · · · · · · · · · · ·

Tuesday 1st

If it feels like you are doing too much, you probably are.
You may feel drained by your social groups or feel that you
are in too deep with something unusual, which doesn't quite
fit your needs. This may cause you to rebel or have a tantrum.

Wednesday 2nd

You may find yourself yearning for something from the past
today; a lost love, a self-care practice or some other desire that
once made you feel good. These are not emotions you can deal
with easily, so give yourself time and space. Hold your inner
child with love.

Thursday 3rd

Searching for a connection with spiritual groups may help you
come back to your centre. Although the territory is unfamiliar
to you, there is comfort to be had with empathic and sensitive
people. You may learn something about a part of you that has
been suppressed. Be gentle with yourself now.

Friday 4th

Your inner compass is being dangled right in front of your
eyes, but it seems more like an illusion. You don't have the
energy to pursue it yet. Use this time to evaluate other things
in your life that connect you to the collective. Listen to your
elders and respect what they have to say.

Saturday 5th

Your energy picks up and you enjoy the comfort of your home and family. Friendship groups may experience some unrest, so stay away if you can. A past love may reappear; perhaps you have brought them back into your consciousness. Deal with them kindly, but keep them in the past.

Sunday 6th

Messages from the past continue to fill your mind. You must let this go. There is part of you that is reluctant to do this, but for your own sanity and self-respect, you must. You know that it's the right thing to do and that it needs to be done lovingly.

Monday 7th

Romance or creativity appear to be the best activities for you today. However, your friendship groups may be making noises that require your attention. Perhaps you have unfinished business to attend to. Make sure you have relaxation time to take care of your own needs. Eat your favourite foods.

Tuesday 8th

The eclipse season closes with a full moon lunar eclipse in your romance sector. This can be a troublesome time and you may find it difficult to communicate your desires. There may be volatile energy that you need to deal with before finally closing the door on something emotional.

Wednesday 9th

Be very careful what you say today as you may upset someone and cause unnecessary conflict. You could experience ego clashes and wild tempers. It's possible that you act out of the ordinary or rebel against your friendship groups. Lovers will feel the brunt of your outburst today.

Thursday 10th

You may be tempted to isolate yourself and switch off from the drama around you. Maybe you'll prefer to binge watch a TV show or read a good book today, but be careful not to over-indulge in anything unhealthy for you. Make sure you stay level-headed.

Friday 11th

Check in with your body, as your health may be suffering. Your stress levels may be higher than usual. You might also be doing too much for other people and becoming a people pleaser. Learn to delegate or say no if you feel you are being put upon.

Saturday 12th

As the weekend arrives, you have a need to be looked after by a special person. This may be a romantic partner, but could also be a mother figure. You desire to feel safe and nurtured. Home-cooked family favourites may take you down a path of nostalgia, which will be good for your soul.

Sunday 13th

Use the lovely energy today to connect with a loved one. You are usually too afraid to show your vulnerability, but let today be the day that you relax in another's company and appreciate what they can do for you. It may surprise you to learn how nice this is.

Monday 14th

A little devil on your shoulder gives you a momentary feeling of manipulation. This is the control freak inside you. Don't listen to it and continue to enjoy being cared for. Intimacy can deepen, if you stop your ego leading the way.

Tuesday 15th

The energy today may have you at a standstill. You don't know
where to go next. Do you have to go anywhere? Can't you be
in the moment without major plans? There may be something
you have overlooked in your friendship arena and this might
involve an ex-partner.

Wednesday 16th

Communication is paramount over the next few days.
Your heart and mind are locked in battle as you wrestle with
ghosts from the past and your feelings towards them. This is a
hurdle that you need to deal with before it eats you up. Stare it
in the face and begin healing.

Thursday 17th

Get your thinking head on now and try to use logic and reason
to fathom an emotional problem. You may be more used to
using hard facts than feelings, so go with what you know.
A lot of this can be done alone, with no outside distractions.

Friday 18th

Let yourself be surprised with how much you can look at
the bigger picture now. This is helpful when attempting to
deal with unfamiliar feelings. You may also find that you can
appreciate the point of view of another and see a different
angle. You can crack this.

Saturday 19th

You must do all you can to remain balanced and fair today.
There is tricky energy around, which may completely drain
you and make you ill. Refuse anything that is not in your best
interests. If you have the urge to talk with a lover, do so, and
you may be pleasantly surprised by their input.

Sunday 20th

A quiet Sunday is welcomed and your sense of equilibrium returns. Enjoy the peace today and remember this feeling. You may want to go off and do something productive, but your health will thank you for simply having a relaxing end to the weekend.

Monday 21st

You may be closing a chapter with social groups due to a jealous or nasty incident. Someone may have revealed their true colours recently. Egos may be bruised but will be healed as soon as the bitter aftertaste has gone. Listen carefully to your heart's desires tonight.

Tuesday 22nd

As you let something or someone go from your life, it is not without grief or regret. This very act may stir up past hurts. Acknowledge them and take a sidestep; there's no need to get embroiled in that all over again. Say goodbye to old habits and move towards adopting better ones.

Wednesday 23rd

It's possible that you must be cruel to be kind today. You may be putting up borders where there were none. This is a great act of self-protection and a very necessary one. Your world may feel too small for you now, but think of it as a cocoon before you grow into something new.

Thursday 24th

A new moon is a chance to wipe the slate clean and start again. Giant Jupiter turns direct at the same time and he will bring you many benefits when you wish upon this moon. This is a wonderful day to express your needs and desires.

Friday 25th

If you are feeling very tired today, take a break. No Friday night parties for you. You may have been pushed to your limit and now need to recharge. Have a night under the duvet with a good book and a hot drink. Ignore the outside world and indulge yourself.

Saturday 26th

A good night's sleep may have been just what you needed. Today's planetary energy is very quiet and giving you some space. This may be a day of reminiscing with close friends and family, or looking through old photos. You may be remembering skills and talents you once enjoyed.

Sunday 27th

Inspiration can come from the oddest of sources. You may find this today and set about creating or transforming something. This could even be a new look for yourself. Whatever you put your mind to today will be blessed with good fortune and be larger than life itself.

Monday 28th

You may not find it easy to settle into the working week. You would rather have stayed at home, doing what was making you happy. However, a few grumbles throughout the day are nothing major to deal with. Get your head down and do your duties. You will be home again soon.

Tuesday 29th

Your mood has picked up and you may sail through the day doing your duties. You are more than happy to help others. You may need to get a few things off your chest this evening and this could be tricky. Do it with kindness and sensitivity.

Wednesday 30th

Take note at what your dream messages tell you. Your intuition is high right now. There is a chance that you can sweet-talk the boss into letting you do something that will enhance your financial and professional status. Hold that thought. Another step up the corporate ladder is exactly what you like.

DECEMBER

· · · · · · · · · · · · · · · · ·

Thursday 1st

Today, you find it impossible to please everyone. Be on the lookout for conflict between men and women. You may not be involved, but could be in the difficult position of holding both parties at bay. This will drain your resources. Step away and let them deal with it by themselves.

Friday 2nd

Whatever your emotions are today, they will be larger than usual. It may not take much to make you elated or to tip you over the edge. You may need to look at your relationship with money and how you are using it. Invest in a wise project or you could watch your cash flow disappear.

Saturday 3rd

You have the energy and drive to deal with family issues today. You are quite aware of your duties here and it pleases you to bring harmony to your clan. Ensure that you know when enough is enough and you are not being asked to do too much.

Sunday 4th

Neptune turns direct today. This is great as you will slowly but surely be able to see your true north once more. However, this may upset the current harmony in the homestead as you become more insular and want your own way. Control and power struggles may surface.

Monday 5th

Check in with any groups where you have a shared spiritual interest. You may have missed something that now needs your attention. Today is also another reset for you. Now that you have full control of your inner compass, you must decide what is attainable and what isn't, then go for it.

Tuesday 6th

There may be a last-minute trigger coming from your deepest psyche. A little word here or there may upset you more than you care to admit. Heal this small wound once and for all. You are yearning to begin the vision quest you have in mind, free from past hurts.

Wednesday 7th

Today, you have a rare chance to sit and do nothing at all. You may choose to spend it as downtime or to do some research, but it will be equally well spent letting another guide your day. This is a day when you feel content and that is unusual for you.

Thursday 8th

A full moon today may show that you need to pay more attention to your health. This can be a draining lunation as you will also see issues about how your routine activities need to be changed or delegated. Health first and everything else comes after.

. . . .

Friday 9th

Today you need to give yourself a pep talk. How might you practise more self-care? Make plans in your schedule to do what fuels your passion and feeds your soul. There may be a course of higher education out there with your name on it. Talk with a loved one about this.

Saturday 10th

Venus enters your sign today to support you with looking after your needs. Again, you may find that a partner knows better than you and you may need to relinquish control. Allow yourself to be treated and nurtured. You may be very surprised at the relaxing effect it has on you.

Sunday 11th

Sharing a dream with a loved one may not be a bad idea. They will give you a lot of support and encouragement. Enjoy a pleasant day of connecting and by evening you may find that you are on a new level. Celebrate with laughter.

Monday 12th

It might feel like a challenge to begin another round of weekly obligations as your current mood is not on the job. Your energy wants to reach outwards, but you feel safer keeping things to yourself for now. This is ego talking, as you are afraid of being knocked back.

Tuesday 13th

Restless energy can make you irritable today. Try to use this up in a different way. Physical exercise may do the trick. You have a need for activity and for your plans to be initiated. Be warned that doing too much can drain you, so take it slowly. One step at a time.

Wednesday 14th

Today may be your first opportunity to show Venus that you are looking after yourself. Think about something you can do that makes you feel good. You could find a situation that involves sharing skills with someone and making a mutually beneficial agreement. That's a great start.

Thursday 15th

The planetary energy is full of grounded earth today. This is great news for you, and this may be your chance to plant your seeds or start manifesting your wishes. Put your thinking cap on and see what you come up with. You may be more inventive than usual.

Friday 16th

Your dreams can be difficult to catch today. Don't try too hard as this will pass soon. There are other more urgent things that need your attention now. This will irritate you, but will free you up to dream when the time is right. Just tick things off your list today.

Saturday 17th

You may slip up today and miss a chance to take care of your needs. It may be that you are working overtime before the festive season arrives. You might have a lot of messages or trips to make this weekend, so be careful that you don't get burnt out.

. . . .

Sunday 18th

This weekend is so full of small jobs that you may have not had time to yourself. However, this shouldn't bother you so much because the jobs have been important and needed to get done. You might have an hour or two to unwind before bedtime, so use it wisely.

Monday 19th

Today, you can make up for any lost time over the weekend. You might book a hair or beauty appointment, or dine out with a friend. What a nice way to start the week. One of your friends may have a treat for you, even if it is simply great conversation.

Tuesday 20th

People may be playing catch up with you today as your energy levels are on fire. You might be very single-minded because you wish to focus on one thing at a time. You could be feeling uplifted and optimistic about the future now.

Wednesday 21st

The Sun enters your sign, so happy birthday! The winter solstice arrives today. The longest night is a chance to pause and reflect on the year gone by and to prepare for the remaining winter months. You may find that you are more introspective now. Slow down and find your calm.

Thursday 22nd

Tensions are rising and you may find that everyone around you is running around like lunatics. The focus now is on what needs to be done. Play can come later. Your general mood is good as you are being steadily productive and that pleases you.

Friday 23rd

A new moon arrives in your sign today. This is the best chance you are going to get to make resolutions, goals and intentions about yourself. Think of your strong work ethic, your status, your morals and how you might appear to others. This is about you and no one else. Make a wish to the universe.

Saturday 24th

This can be an exciting day for many reasons. You have time for yourself and do something that delights you. There is also time to converse from the heart with others and share your dreams. You may spend the day with your favourite person or being good to yourself.

Sunday 25th

The planets rejoice and spread goodwill. You communicate your deepest wishes with ease and get support from those you love. You sense that a big change is on the way. The mood around you is happy, loving and optimistic. Enjoy your day.

Monday 26th

Be careful that you don't overdo the food and alcohol.
You may be so involved with groups that your one-to-one
relationships suffer. Try to make time for a rendezvous with
your lover. Also, be mindful that you can't please everyone
all the time. Step back if you need to.

Tuesday 27th

A little respite from this busy season might be a good thing
today. You may prefer to spend some time in solitude and
switch off before the festivities start up again. If you have a
spiritual practice, that may help you find your centre again.

Wednesday 28th

Stay in your own space for now. The energy is giving you time
to dream and look after yourself. If you communicate this to
your nearest and dearest, they will understand. Treat yourself
to your favourite food, entertainment and, if you wish, time
with someone you trust and love a great deal.

Thursday 29th

Just as you think you're in the clear, Mercury turns retrograde
in your sign. Be careful with travel plans and slow right down.
Double-check everything, be precise with communication and
back up all technical devices. Always put yourself first.

Friday 30th

There is tricky energy to deal with today. If it's possible, stay at
home. If you must go out, take a walk as this will give you the
downtime you need in this hectic season.

Saturday 31st

This final day of 2022 is filled with a few challenges. These could range from not having enough time to do your self-care routines, to wondering about who will host the best party tonight. Will you even go out at all? Or will you stay in with a loved one? Do what feels best for you.

Capricorn

....

PEOPLE WHO SHARE
YOUR SIGN

PEOPLE WHO
SHARE YOUR SIGN
. . . .

Dignified, self-sufficient and determined, the perseverance and patience of Capricorns makes them often take first place in whatever they set their mind to. Take the King of Rock, Elvis Presley and world-renowned physicist Stephen Hawking as just two examples of what the persevering Capricorn can achieve. Discover which of these established Capricorns share your exact birthday and see if you can spot the similarities.

22nd December
Meghan Trainor (1993), Shiori Kutsuna (1992), Jordin Sparks (1989), Chris Carmack (1980), Vanessa Paradis (1972), Dina Meyer (1968), Ralph Fiennes (1962), Jean-Michel Basquiat (1960), Héctor Elizondo (1936)

23rd December
Harry Judd (1985), Jodie Marsh (1978), Corey Haim (1971), Carla Bruni (1967), Eddie Vedder (1964), Dave Murray (1956), Carol Ann Duffy (1955), Emperor Akihito of Japan (1933), Madam C. J. Walker (1867), Joseph Smith (1805)

24th December
Louis Tomlinson (1991), Ryan Seacrest (1974), Stephenie Meyer (1973), Ricky Martin (1971), Ed Miliband (1969), Kate Spade (1962), Carol Vorderman (1960), Lemmy Kilmister (1945), Ava Gardner (1922), Howard Hughes (1905), Empress Elisabeth of Austria (1837)

25th December

Hailie Jade (1995), Armin van Buuren (1976), Dido (1971),
Justin Trudeau, Canadian Prime Minister (1971), Annie
Lennox (1954), Sissy Spacek (1949), Jimmy Buffett (1946),
Humphrey Bogart (1899), Muhammad Ali Jinnah, Founder
of Pakistan (1876), Clara Barton (1821)

26th December

Eden Sher (1991), Andy Biersack (1990), Aaron Ramsey (1990),
Kit Harington (1986), Hugo Lloris (1986), Beth Behrs (1985),
Alexander Wang (1983), Jared Leto (1971), Lars Ulrich (1963),
David Sedaris (1956)

27th December

Olivia Cooke (1993), Hayley Williams (1988), Lily Cole (1987),
Emilie de Ravin (1981), Salman Khan (1965), Gérard Depardieu
(1948), John Amos (1939), Marlene Dietrich (1901)

28th December

Sienna Miller (1981), Noomi Rapace (1979), John Legend
(1978), Joe Manganiello (1976), Seth Meyers (1973), Denzel
Washington (1954), Maggie Smith (1934), Stan Lee (1922),
Woodrow Wilson, U.S. President (1856)

29th December

Dylan Minnette (1996), Ross Lynch (1995), Kei Nishikori
(1989), Alison Brie (1982), Charlotte Riley (1981), Diego Luna
(1979), Jude Law (1972), Patricia Clarkson (1959), Ted Danson
(1947), Jon Voight (1938)

30th December

Ellie Goulding (1986), LeBron James (1984), Kristin Kreuk (1982), Eliza Dushku (1980), Tyrese Gibson (1978), Tiger Woods (1975), Patti Smith (1946), Rudyard Kipling (1865)

31st December

Sam Faiers (1990), PSY (1977), Donald Trump Jr. (1977), Nicholas Sparks (1965), Val Kilmer (1959), Donna Summer (1948), Diane von Fürstenberg (1946), John Denver (1943), Ben Kingsley (1943), Alex Ferguson (1941), Anthony Hopkins (1937), King Salman of Saudi Arabia (1935), Henri Matisse (1869)

1st January

Jack Wilshere (1992), Colin Morgan (1986), Paolo Guerrero (1984), Elin Nordegren (1980), Sonali Bendre (1975), Morris Chestnut (1969), Verne Troyer (1969), J.D. Salinger (1919), J. Edgar Hoover (1895)

2nd January

Bryson Tiller (1993), Shelley Hennig (1987), Kate Bosworth (1983), Dax Shepard (1975), Taye Diggs (1971), Christy Turlington (1969), Cuba Gooding Jr. (1968), Tia Carrere (1967)

3rd January

Danica McKellar (1975), Michael Schumacher (1969), Mel Gibson (1956), Victoria Principal (1950), Robert Loggia (1930), Sergio Leone (1929), J. R. R. Tolkien (1892), Savitribai Phule (1831)

4th January

Liza Soberano (1998), Toni Kroos (1990), James Milner (1986), Jeannie Mai (1979), Julia Ormond (1965), Craig Revel Horwood (1965), Dave Foley (1963), Harlan Coben (1962), Michael Stipe (1960), Tina Knowles (1954), Rick Stein (1947)

5th January

Suki Waterhouse (1992), Kristin Cavallari (1987), Deepika Padukone (1986), Deadmau5 (1981), January Jones (1978), Bradley Cooper (1975), Marilyn Manson (1969), Vinnie Jones (1965), Diane Keaton (1946), Hayao Miyazaki (1941)

6th January

MattyBRaps (2003), Irina Shayk (1986), Alex Turner (1986), Kate McKinnon (1984), Eddie Redmayne (1982), Norman Reedus (1969), Nigella Lawson (1960), Kahlil Gibran (1883)

7th January

Eden Hazard (1991), Hardwell (1988), Lewis Hamilton (1985), Lauren Cohan (1982), Vybz Kartel (1976), Jeremy Renner (1971), Irrfan Khan (1967), Nicolas Cage (1964), Christian Louboutin (1963)

8th January

Noah Cyrus (2000), David Bowie (1947), Stephen Hawking (1942), Carolina Herrera (1939), Shirley Bassey (1937), Elvis Presley (1935)

9th January

Nicola Peltz (1995), Nina Dobrev (1989), Kate Middleton,
Duchess of Cambridge (1982), Omari Hardwick (1974), Sean
Paul (1973), Joely Richardson (1965), J. K. Simmons (1955),
Jimmy Page (1944), Richard Nixon, U.S. President (1913),
Simone de Beauvoir (1908)

10th January

Abbey Clancy (1986), Jared Kushner (1981), Cash Warren
(1979), Jemaine Clement (1974), Maurizio Sarri (1959),
Pat Benatar (1953), George Foreman (1949), Rod Stewart
(1945)

11th January

Cody Simpson (1997), Leroy Sané (1996), Jamie Vardy (1987),
Rachel Riley (1986), Amanda Peet (1972), Mary J. Blige (1971),
Kyle Richards (1969), Yolanda Hadid (1964), Alice Paul (1885)

12th January

Zayn Malik (1993), Naya Rivera (1987), Raf Simons (1968),
Rob Zombie (1965), Jeff Bezos (1964), Howard Stern (1954),
Kirstie Alley (1951), Haruki Murakami (1949), Swami
Vivekananda (1863)

13th January

Liam Hemsworth (1990), Julian Morris (1983), Ruth Wilson
(1982), Orlando Bloom (1977), Michael Peña (1976), Nicole
Eggert (1972), Patrick Dempsey (1966), Julia Louis-Dreyfus
(1961), Janet Hubert (1956)

14th January

Grant Gustin (1990), Yandel (1977), Jason Bateman (1969),
Dave Grohl (1969), LL Cool J (1968), Zakk Wylde (1967),
Carl Weathers (1948), Holland Taylor (1943)

15th January

Dove Cameron (1996), Skrillex (1988), Kelly Kelly (1987),
Pitbull (1981), Regina King (1971), Shane McMahon (1970),
Martin Luther King Jr. (1929)

16th January

FKA twigs (1988), Nick Valensi (1981), Lin-Manuel Miranda
(1980), Aaliyah (1979), Kate Moss (1974), Roy Jones Jr. (1969),
John Carpenter (1948), René Angélil (1942)

17th January

Calvin Harris (1984), Ray J (1981), Zooey Deschanel (1980),
Tiësto (1969), Michelle Obama (1964), Jim Carrey (1962),
Muhammad Ali (1942), James Earl Jones (1931), Betty White
(1922), Al Capone (1899)

18th January

Karan Brar (1999), Angelique Kerber (1988), Jason Segel
(1980), Pep Guardiola (1971), Dave Bautista (1969), Mark
Rylance (1960), Kevin Costner (1955), Cary Grant (1904)

19th January

Logan Lerman (1992), Mac Miller (1992), Claudio Marchisio (1986), Utada Hikaru (1983), Jenson Button (1980), Ricardo Arjona (1964), Dolly Parton (1946), Janis Joplin (1943), Edgar Allan Poe (1809)

20th January

Evan Peters (1987), Joe Swash (1982), Mark Wright (1981), Gary Barlow (1971), Stacey Dash (1967), Rainn Wilson (1966), Bill Maher (1956), Paul Stanley (1952), David Lynch (1946), Dorothy Provine (1935), Tom Baker (1934), Buzz Aldrin (1930), Federico Fellini (1920)